Evolution and Eden

Balancing Original Sin and Contemporary Science

Jerry D. Korsmeyer

PAULIST PRESS
New York / Mahwah, N.J.

Cover art entitled *Original Sin and Expulsion from Paradise* by Michelangelo Buonarroti (ceiling fresco from the Sistine Chapel, Vatican Palace, Vatican State). Used courtesy of Scala/Art Resource, NY.

The Publisher gratefully acknowledges use of the following: Excerpts from *The Basic Writings of Saint Augustine,* Vol. II, edited by Whitney J. Oates. Copyright 1948 by Random House, Inc. Reprinted by permission of Random House, Inc., and by permission of T&T Clark Ltd. Publishers.

Cover design by Cindy Dunne

Library of Congress Cataloging-in-Publication Data

Korsmeyer, Jerry D.
    Evolution and Eden : balancing original sin and contemporary science / Jerry D. Korsmeyer.
        p.   cm.
    Includes bibliographical references and index.
    ISBN 0–8091–3815–8 (alk. paper)
    1. Sin, Original. 2. Evolution—Religious aspects—Catholic Church. 3. Catholic Church—Doctrines. I. Title.
BT720.K67   1998
233′.14—dc21   98–28968
                                                                              CIP

Published by Paulist Press
997 Macarthur Boulevard
Mahwah, New Jersey 07430

www.paulistpress.com

Printed and bound in the
United States of America

Contents

Preface

This book is about an interface between science and religion, and a very crucial one for Catholicism. How the Church finally comes to grips with the question of human origins will significantly affect its relationship to an ever more educated world. The Church's current stance toward evolution is ambivalent. In some quarters there are positive signs and statements. In other areas the evidence is downright fundamentalist and anti-evolution. The presence of some serious doctrinal problem is evident, and the need to solve it is becoming great. I would like to believe that the recent statement of Pope John Paul II, where he said that evolution is more than just a hypothesis, is a plea for theologians and scientists to get on with it and provide a modern Catholic perspective on evolution.[1]

One thinks of the saying about fools rushing in. But Vatican II invited theologically trained scientists to speak up on these topics.[2] And one of Catholicism's finest theologians, Karl Rahner, S.J., urged the new generation of theologians not to be afraid to tackle the big topics.[3] This one is big. It concerns the Church's understanding of what revelation really is. It concerns how the Church interprets Scripture, and it concerns, especially, the dogma of original sin.

I am convinced that the great theologians of the Church, if

1

they were alive today, would be actively synthesizing modern scientific and philosophical knowledge with the good news of the Gospel. As Augustine used Platonism, and Aquinas the teaching of Aristotle, so today the faith can benefit from our scientific knowledge of the universe, and from the insights of process philosophy. Listen to what a doctor of the early Church has to say about science and Christianity.

> Usually, even a non-Christian knows something about the earth, the heavens, and the other elements of this world, about the motion and orbit of the stars, and even their size and relative positions, about the predictable eclipses of the sun and moon, the cycles of the years and the seasons, about the kinds of animals, shrubs, stones, and so forth, and this knowledge he holds to as being certain from reason and experience. Now it is a disgraceful and dangerous thing for an infidel to hear a Christian, presumably giving the meaning of Holy Scripture, talking nonsense on these topics; and we should take all means to prevent such an embarrassing situation, in which people show up vast ignorance in a Christian and laugh it to scorn.[4]

Yes, this is St. Augustine—the same Augustine whose theory of original sin is taught in the new *Catechism of the Catholic Church,* a theory that proposes as literal truth the creation of the first humans with advanced knowledge and not subject to suffering or death.

I intend to examine the history of the Church's interaction with the concept of evolution and the development of the doctrine of original sin. Then I will suggest an interpretation of original sin in keeping with modern Catholic scholarship and modern scientific knowledge.

To date, most Catholic theologians have restricted themselves to the theological questions brought up by evolution. Except for a few popularizers, scientists have limited themselves to the scientific results of their investigations, which is all their discipline supports. It was rare in the past that any theologian grappled with the scientific results on evolution (Teilhard de Chardin and Karl Rahner come to mind). It was even rarer that any scientists were knowledgeable enough to ask the right theological questions, or to understand the historical origin of the Church's positions. Communication has been hindered by a widespread impression among Christians that scientists are mostly atheists, or otherwise anti-religious.

In over thirty years of work, as a physicist and engineering manager at a United States Department of Energy laboratory, it was my experience that most American scientists and engineers are quite religious. While being trained as a theologian, the impression was received that few theologians feel comfortable addressing scientific subjects, although that is now changing.[5] Differences in understanding and approach between scientists and theologians are part of the problem in the case of evolution. They have helped to create the mystery that now faces the man and woman in the pew. This book is an attempt to throw some light on the situation, and to advance theological anthropology by proposing an interpretation of evolution and original sin in creative fidelity to the Catholic faith.

It is a pleasure to acknowledge that my work has been enriched by long conversations on many of the topics discussed here, while vacationing at the beach with Joe and Joanne Kepes. They also carefully reviewed drafts of some early chapters. I would also like to thank Kathleen Walsh of Paulist Press for her support, and for her guidance in shaping the book's content. And, of course, the whole project would have been impossible without the steady encouragement and editorial eye of my wife, Mary Gail.

Introduction
Evolution: Favored or Feared?

In a patter-song from Gilbert and Sullivan's "Mikado," a haughty high official is made to say that he can trace his ancestry all the way back to a "protoplasmal primordial atomic globule." It now appears that he was correct. And we all can do the same, tracing the origin of our atoms to the interior of stars which burned themselves out billions of years ago.

Pope John Paul II has several times in recent years indicated his conviction that evolution is more than just a theory, and has speculated upon possible new insights that knowledge of the formation of the universe may provide for the understanding of Christian doctrines. The Vatican itself has for some years now been sponsoring a regular series of conferences between scientists and theologians on a variety of subjects of interest to both science and religion, subjects such as evolution.[1]

Yet, for the Catholic, there is an aura of mystery surrounding the whole subject of evolution. An attempt to determine the official Catholic position on the subject uncovers only a few tentative official statements expressing partial approval and deep concern. In the new *Catechism of the Catholic Church,* the story of Adam and Eve from Genesis 1–11 is presented as historical truth.[2] Theologians and Scripture scholars were confused by this, since Vatican II had clearly affirmed the use of historical critical methods when interpreting the Bible.

It seems that official Church pronouncements on original sin, made in an earlier period of history at the Council of Trent, provide a difficult challenge for those who would produce a modern interpretation. In defending itself against the Protestants, the Church at Trent reaffirmed, in passing, the ancient Augustinian formulation of "original sin." Adam the first man was originally created holy and just. By his sin, which was a crime so cataclysmic that the whole human race was alienated from God, he and his descendants were changed in their very natures, and made subject to suffering, physical death, and death of the soul unless redeemed by the grace of God. The guilt of this original fault is taken away by baptism while concupiscence remains. Newborn infants require baptism for the remission of sin to attain eternal life.

How was this to be reinterpreted in the new *Catechism*, to bring out the truth contained therein, separated from its culturally conditioned aspects? The question was filled with troublesome ramifications: Augustine's view of original sin, the problem of evil, and the Church's investment in the immutable God of Greek philosophy.

When the curial commission responsible for *Catechism* was pressed, it became clear that they were unsure how to handle the doctrine of "original sin." *Catechism*'s Editorial Secretary, Christoph Schönborn, stated:

> A particularly delicate subject is original sin. A special commission had occupied itself at length with the formulation of this segment. It cannot be the task of the Catechism to represent novel theological theses which do not belong to the assured patrimony of the Church's faith. Consequently, the Catechism limits itself to setting forth the sure doctrine of the faith.[3]

As a result, the story of Adam and Eve is presented in Catechism as history, and, while the attentive reader will see occasional reference to the "symbolism" of biblical language, it is made clear that the whole of nature was originally in a state of "original justice," of harmony with God, such that there was no suffering or death. Because of Adam and Eve's disobedience, original justice was lost and "visible creation has become alien and hostile to man."[4] *Catechism* then goes on to give what is essentially Augustine's concept of "original sin." Because of Adam's sin, which is propagated to all humans sexually, all are punished by evil, suffering and death, both physical and spiritual. Because of this second "death of the soul," all require redemption.

There is no specific mention of the possibility that the universe and human nature have evolved. Neither the word "evolution" nor the concept is mentioned.[5] Gabriel Daly, OSA, from Trinity College, Dublin, a distinguished expert on creation and original sin, recognizes the serious implications of *Catechism*'s stance.

> At this point we enter a zone of serious theological problems which will in turn be reflected in equally serious catechetical problems. Nearly all of these problems stem from the difficulty of reconciling the pre-critical view of the Genesis stories with our contemporary knowledge of (a) the physical and biological origins of the human race; (b) the literary genre of the book of Genesis; and (c) the impossibility of conceiving of an actual *historical* 'original state of holiness and justice' (375) in which there was no pain or death.
>
> The question which has arisen at several points in the teaching of the *Catechism* on creation now becomes insistent and unavoidable in the context of its teaching on original justice and the fall. The first three chapters of Genesis, we are told, 'occupy a unique place' and 'remain the principal source for catechesis on the mysteries of the "beginning": creation, fall, and promise of salvation' (289).[6]

As a result of this presentation in *Catechism,* Catholics are faced with a number of questions that challenge their faith. Is evolution now favored or feared? One can see that there have been two differing trends in Catholic thought on this subject. To unravel the situation we need to go back to earlier questions. What has been the history of the Church's response to evolution? What are the theological problems, and how has the Church dealt with them? How do our bishops understand the relationship between science and religion? How does Augustine's interpretation of Scripture and the faith pass muster today?

In light of the blossoming of biblical studies and theology since Vatican II, what do the biblical scholars and the theologians have to say about the interpretation of Genesis and the concept of original sin? Can Catholic theology come up with an interpretation that makes the faith more credible than the Adam and Eve story as history? Does the Catholic faith require belief in a world that was once without pain and death? And then there are questions about evolution itself.

What about evolution? Is evolution really at question as a scientific theory today? It appears that the public may think so. Gallop polls in recent years have shown that half the American people believe that humans were directly created within the last ten thousand years.[7] In fact, the number of people who believe this has gone up in recent years. What's going on? A brief foray into the current debates on evolution and its status from a scientific point of view is in order.

Suppose, for the sake of argument, that it was certain that the whole universe evolved over billions of years, and that humanity evolved from lower forms of life. The billions of years of divine activity creating life before the first conscious being walked the earth are not part of our religious tradition. With what purpose, to what end were these things done? What does divine action in evolution of the universe tell us? Doesn't nature, as Aquinas said, reveal something of the Creator? Could God's way of working with the world be a clue to something about the divine nature? Could the divine nature itself be different somehow from what we have assumed?

The Church needs a theology of evolution. We shall suggest a framework upon which such a theology could be based. It will require a modification of the Greek philosophy implicit in official Roman theology today. We need a theology that makes sense of evolution, that provides a way of considering it that fits with our view of the Creator. We need a worldview that casts light upon a God who creates in an evolutionary fashion. This theology needs to be consistent with Scripture's portrayal of a loving God. This theology also needs to assure us that a world filled with excessive natural evil is consistent with the all-pervading presence of a God who is worthy of worship.

Having outlined such a theology, we will look at its implications for the doctrine of original sin. What did the millions of years of human evolution provide as biological and cultural inheritance for our ancestors as they first became conscious of themselves and of God? Did they fall into self-consciousness from a state of alienation from the divine?

These questions will be discussed, with the intent of providing confidence that there is no real opposition between science and theology, and that there is no reason to fear the theory of evolution. It will become apparent that Catholic theologians have been aware of this for years—that ample studies on original sin provide a variety of interpretations consistent with the faith, and not in opposition to modern science.

Some new thoughts on the reasons for past theological problems in the area of original sin will be offered, along with a neoclassical or process view of original sin that is consonant with modern science and with the deep convictions of the Catholic tradition.

Finally, it will be suggested that, rather than being a problem, knowledge of evolution is a "sign of our times," and, as such, a key to a new understanding of the divine and its working in our lives. We worship a living God, one who continues to reveal God's self to us. The future is full of the lure and call of divine love. What we need is creative transformation of Catholic doctrine, inspired by the Spirit, and worked out through the cooperation of the hierarchial, theological and scientific callings of the people of God.

1
The Church and Evolution— A Brief History

Evolution did not begin with Darwin. The general idea that the world or some of its parts have undergone irreversible, cumulative changes, such that the number, variety, and complexity of its parts have increased, has been traced as far back as Confucius, early Buddhism and the pre-Socratics.[1] Anaximander believed that humans first developed in some fish-like creature and later emerged to live on dry land. Democritus held some ideas of social and cultural evolution. Humans first lived like individual animals, he stated, but gathered together for mutual protection and comfort. It wasn't until Plato and Aristotle that anti-evolutionary concepts came to the fore and dominated Western thought for more than a millennium.

Plato (428–348 B.C.) with his real world of unchanging forms saw the visible world as made up of imperfect copies of ideal archetypes that could never change. His ultimate concept, the "Good," was totally self-sufficient, and, through a lesser power, the Demiurge, it created all creatures because "in one that is good no envy of anything else arises. Being devoid of envy, then, he desired that everything should be as far as possible like himself."[2]

After establishing this reason for creation, Plato goes on in *Timaeus* to answer the question: What kinds of creatures must the world contain? The answer: All kinds, because nothing incomplete is good.[3] This idea of the realization in actuality of the fullness of conceptional possibility is called the "principle of plenitude." It has had a major influence on Christian theology.[4] Aristotle (384–322 B.C.) had a slightly modified view. He held that it was not necessary for everything that was possible to be actual, and he suggested to later naturalists that animals should be ranked in a scale according to their perfection.[5] From Plato and Aristotle it took only a few steps to get these ideas firmly into Christian theology. Plato's views were taken up by the neo-Platonists, particularly by Plotinus (A.D. 205–270), and Plotinus was studied by Augustine. The neo-Platonic conception of the universe as a Great Chain of Being composed of an immense, or infinite, number of links, ranging in hierarchical order from the smallest existing things through every possible grade up to the highest possible creature, was accepted by most educated people from the middle ages to the late eighteenth century.[6] These ideas passed into Christian cosmology and theology through Augustine (A.D. 354–430) and Pseudo-Dionysius the Aeropagite, the supposed Athenian disciple of St. Paul (c. A.D. 500). The latter spoke of creatures flowing from the superabundance of God's goodness, and Augustine incorporated the principle of plenitude into his book *The City of God*. He writes:

> And if God, as Plato continually maintains, embraced in His eternal intelligence the ideas both of the universe and of all the animals, how, then, should He not with His own hand make them all? Could He be unwilling to be the constructor of works, the idea and plan of which called for His ineffable and ineffably to be praised intelligence?[7]

Augustine struggled throughout his life as a bishop to produce a book on the interpretation of Genesis.[8] By the "literal" meaning of Genesis, Augustine meant "what actually happened," rather than the typological, prophetic, or allegorical meaning. By the term "literal" he did not mean "what the words commonly mean," but what facts they refer to, and how they could be interpreted to be consistent with the whole of Scripture, producing a non-contradictory presentation. For example, since Genesis says that God created the heavens and earth, and then describes creation in six days, Augustine concluded that everything was created all at once, and that "seed principles" were created to cause creatures to appear at different times in accordance with the observations of nature.[9] Thus, the "days" of creation were really categories arranged by the author to assist explanation. In trying to make consistent every phrase of the dual creation accounts in Genesis, he concluded, among other things, that since "light" is mentioned before creation of the sun and stars, it refers to the spiritual illumination of the angels.

The second major entry of Greek philosophical thought into Christian theology came through Aquinas (A.D. 1224–1274). He was inventive in finding multiple reasons why God created a multitude of creatures.

> But all goodness possessed by creatures is finite, falling short of the infinite goodness of God. Hence, the universe of creatures is more perfect if there are many grades of things than if there were but one. Now, it befits the supreme good to make what is best. It was therefore fitting that God should make many grades of creatures.[10]

Aquinas reaffirmed the principle of plenitude, with a modification following Aristotle, that while God conceived of an infinite number of possible things, not all are chosen for existence.[11]

These ideas, taken from the Greek philosophers, were repeated for centuries when the educated spoke of nature and God's creation. Little, if any, development in evolutionary thinking occurred between Augustine and Descartes in the sixteenth century. "The static creationism associated with Christian biblical studies made it difficult for any idea of evolution to arise, let alone be defended."[12] Natural philosophy (what today we call science) was largely mixed in with scriptural exegesis. As one scholar notes:

> Between the fifth and the thirteenth centuries little attention was paid to the science of nature in its own right. It is in the "hexemeral" literature (commentaries on the work of the six days) that one finds an account of the natural knowledge of the day. The Genesis story of origins provided the occasion for an orderly review of what was known of the heavens, the earth, the plant world, the animal world, and the nature of man. It did not seem important to stress the difference between the two sources of knowledge, the Bible and experience, since both came from God. Encyclopedists like Isidore of Seville moved easily from one source to the other in their chapters on nature. And Augustine's cosmogony continued to find favor. The origin of kinds was thought of not as a discontinuous series of divine interventions over a period of six days but as a gradual unfolding of potencies set within the original matter by God.[13]

Before Western culture moved on to evolutionary evidence and theories, there was a peak period where the Greek ideas of "plenitude" reigned. During this period Copernicus showed that the earth was not the center of the universe; it revolved around the sun. The interest of educated people turned to speculation about the heavens. The neo-Platonic ideas of plenitude began to be applied to theories of the cosmos. It became widely held that the stars were suns like our own, and had inhabited planets, for the goodness of God demanded that creatures be created wherever possible. The philosophical thought of Cusanus, Giordano Bruno, and Leibniz also supported the concept of the Great Chain of Being. This concept, as noted above, envisioned the universe as an ordered hierarchy of creatures, from the lowest to the highest, even to the *ens perfectissimum,* the end to which all creatures tend.[14] In the eighteenth century, men of science, philosophers, poets and popular essayists, deists, and orthodox divines all talked about the Great Chain of Being, and accepted its implications. Humans were the "middle link" between the merely sentient and the intellectual beings. But the existence of fixed steps in the Chain meant that there could be no advance for humanity, and no change to the evils present in the world. It was the best of all possible worlds, and thus a drain on human optimism.

A reaction began, which resulted in what philosopher Arthur Lovejoy has called, "The temporalizing of the Chain of Being."[15] By this is meant that the full range of creatures came to be viewed, not as the fixed inventory of the universe but as nature's program for the slow and gradual development of creatures in cosmic time. Note that this was still well before the time of Darwin (1809–1882). Descartes (1596–1650) had proposed a theory of the gradual formation of the universe under natural laws, back in the seventeenth century. Other theories of cosmic origins were set out by the philosopher Kant (1724–1804) and the mathematician Laplace (1749–1827).

The move toward evolution was given a boost by the rise of geology and paleontology. Charles Lyell (1797–1875) proposed that the surface features of the earth are the result of the slow and continuous application of natural forces. The Compte de Buffon (1707–1788) conjectured that the age of the earth is far greater than allowed by biblical chronology, and others speculated that fossils, which had been found since antiquity, were the remains of once living beings. The biological sciences brought forth new thoughts on comparative anatomy, embryology, and genetics, which stimulated an emerging evolutionism. The mathematician Maupertuis (1698–1759) envisioned how species might change. The French encyclopedist Diderot (1713–1784) developed a thoroughgoing materialist theory of development of the universe that underwent endless changes over millions of years.[16] Erasmus Darwin, Charles's grandfather, and Jean Baptiste Lamarck were eighteenth century deists who saw the progression of living things from simple to complex as the actualizing of the divine cosmic plan. All these studies paved the way for Charles Darwin.

Darwin's achievement was to produce a large body of evidence that evolution had actually occurred, and to provide an explanation for how it happened. He made evolution a testable theory. With modifications, it has gained scientific support ever since. But the fact that the theory talked of development of species and perhaps humans themselves, by the action of natural laws, suggested a materialistic or mechanistic system that many saw as a denial of the Creator. The Christian reaction to the concept of evolution, as they envisioned it, was sufficiently swift and strong that Darwin and others, who were convinced by him, were fearful of stating openly the conclusions they drew from his work.

Church Pronouncements

It is noteworthy that the Catholic Church had not condemned evolution per se. In fact, it had been slowly moving toward official acceptance of the concept, with several carefully spelled out reservations. Before looking at those reservations, which go the heart of our story, observe how the few Church documents and papal pronouncements that touch on the subject were, and still are, beginning to speak about evolution in a more positive way.[17]

The Provincial Council of Cologne, in 1860, stated that it was contrary to Scripture and the faith to say that even the human body was produced by spontaneous transformation (a natural change from one species to another), or to say that the whole race did not derive from Adam. Theologians have argued over whether this really condemned evolution. It probably did not, since the condemned concept of spontaneous transformation assumed the absence of a divine Creator, while the theory of evolution, as we shall see, says nothing about a Creator.

Ten years later, at Vatican I (1869–1870), it was anticipated that the Council would define the descendance of all humans from a single couple as a dogma of faith. However, the Council lasted for less than a year, cut short by Pius IX because of the outbreak of the Franco-Prussian war. It never addressed this subject. However, one of the few documents produced by the Council contains some very important statements for the relationship between science and religion, asserting that there can be no real contradiction between faith and reason. The matter is worthy of direct quotation.

> Although faith is above reason, there can never be any real discrepancy between faith and reason, since the same God who reveals mysteries and infuses faith has bestowed the light of reason on the human mind, and God cannot deny himself, nor can truth ever contradict truth. The false appearance of such a contradiction is mainly due, either to the dogma of faith not having been understood and expounded according to the mind of the Church, or to the inventions of opinion having been taken for the verdicts of reason.[18]

In 1909 the Biblical Commission issued a series of statements that insisted upon the literal historical sense for "the special creation of man, the formation of the first woman from the first man, the unity of the human race."[19] Nevertheless, as was authoritatively stated in 1948, the reply of the Biblical Commission did not exclude further research.[20] In 1941, Pope Pius XII, in a talk to the Pontifical Academy of Science, affirmed that there could be no true generation of a human from an inferior creature, and insisted that woman has come forth from man.[21] This was interpreted to mean, however, that while the soul was created directly by God, there might still be a *physical* link between an inferior creature and humans.

The big step forward came with Pius XII's encyclical *Humani Generis* (1950), a document that is still today the most important statement of the Catholic Church on the subject. For the first time a "doctrine of evolution" was directly addressed, and there was no talk of the woman originating from man.

> Thus the teaching of the Church leaves the doctrine of evolution an open question, as long as it confines its speculations to the development of the human body from other living matter already in existence. (That souls are immediately created by God is a view which the Catholic faith imposes on us.)....There are other conjectures, about polygenism (as it is called), which leave the faithful no such freedom of debate. Christians cannot lend their support to a theory which involved the existence, after Adam's time, of some earthly race of men, truly so called, who were not descended ultimately from him, or else supposes that Adam was the name given to some group of our primordial ancestors. *It does not appear how such views can be reconciled with the doctrine of original sin,* as this is guaranteed to us by the Church. Original sin is the result of a sin committed, in actual historical fact, by an individual man named Adam, and it is a quality native to all of us, only because it has been handed down by descent from him (Dz 3987).[22] [Italics mine]

Vatican Council II did not come to grips with the subject of human origins, although at least the subject was mentioned in the language of contemporary culture, without condemning it, and it is admitted that the evolutionary ideas of Teilhard de Chardin had "a certain influence, at least indirect, and diffuse, on some orientations of the Council."[23] In the Pastoral Constitution on the Church in the Modern World *(Gaudium et spes),* we read, "And so mankind substitutes a dynamic and more evolutionary concept of nature for a static one" (GS 5). And later in the same document, "historical studies tend to make us view things under the aspects of changeability and evolution" (GS 54).[24] It was not a lot, but it was a step toward recognition of the concept of evolution. There has been a great deal of theologizing since Vatican II that has advanced our understanding of both creation and original sin—so much so that most theologians consider that the objections to evolution could be overcome.[25]

These studies helped produce an atmosphere in which the old wounds between religion and science seemed to be healing. In June 1988, in a message to a group of scientists and theologians gathered by papal invitation at the Vatican Observatory for a Study Week, Pope John Paul II urged scientists and theologians to come to understand each other for their mutual benefit. "Science can purify religion from error and superstition," he said, "religion can purify science from idolatry and false absolutes. Each can draw the other into a wider world, a world in which both can flourish."[26] Further, he spoke of the evolution of the universe, and even speculated upon possible advances from the carry-over of an evolutionary perspective into theology.

> If the cosmologies of the ancient Near Eastern world could be purified and assimilated into the first chapters of Genesis, might contemporary cosmology have something to offer to our reflections upon creation? Does an evolutionary perspective bring any light to bear upon theological anthropology, the meaning of the human person as the *imago Dei,* the problem of Christology—and even upon the development of doctrine itself? What, if any, are the eschatological implications of contemporary cosmology, especially in light of the vast future of our universe? Can theological method fruitfully appropriate insights from scientific methodology and the philosophy of science?[27]

Tentative remarks certainly, but a far cry from the literal biblicism of the past. Finally, in October 1996, Pope John Paul II made a statement on evolution that startled Catholics. He had sponsored, through the Vatican Observatory, a conference on

Evolution and Divine Action in the Universe. After its completion, in a formal address to the Pontifical Academy of Sciences,
he declared that "fresh knowledge" produced by scientific
research now led to the "recognition of the theory of evolution
as more than just a hypothesis." Still, he said, Roman Catholics
must believe that "the spiritual soul is immediately created by
God."[28] What the Pope said was little different from what Pope
Pius XII said forty-six years earlier. What was startling was that
Pope John Paul II just a few years earlier had approved
Catechism, where evolution was not mentioned in discussion of
original sin. We need to understand the serious theological
objections to the theory of evolution.

Key Theological Objections

The roadblocks to theological acceptance of the theory of
evolution are found in *Humani Generis*. The first concerns
the conviction of the special spiritual nature of humanity,
which has been expressed in the insistence that each human
soul is especially created by God. The second, and more
important, is the fear that evolution cannot be reconciled with
the doctrine of original sin, which is viewed as the main reason for the coming of the Savior.

A major theme of the Bible is the special covenant of God
with the human race. Humanity is pictured in Genesis as the
pinnacle of creation, the image of God, and the recipient of a
divine promise. And in the New Testament, the human race is
so special that God sends the only Son to die for us. One can
interpret this to mean that humans are unique, and as the
object of divine love they are called to become God-like, to be
responsible caretakers of our world, and so worthy for eternal
life. Or there is the more anthropocentric view, that humans are
the center of all creation, and were given the universe to domi-
nate for their own use. Of course, the second way neglects the

biblical presentation of the Lord as God of all creation, and forgets that after the flood God told Noah he was establishing a covenant with every living creature. In any case, the uniqueness and special dignity of humanity are concepts that have led to the affirmation of the direct creation of the human soul.

When the theory of evolution was proposed, it was promptly claimed by some that this meant that now a divine creator was needed no longer, since it would be shown that the world could arise from natural processes open to scientific investigation. These investigations would show that humans, body and soul, descended from the lower beasts. Churchmen reacted strongly to these ideas. Human intellect, its sensibilities and free will, could never have derived from the brute animal world, they claimed. The human soul was a spiritual substance, immortal and noble. Here was another product of Platonic influence, the immortal soul. Though the idea is not biblically based, it had been endorsed by the Church, and was now utilized to guarantee the human place as the crown of creation. In direct reaction to the evolutionary claims, the Church proclaimed that God directly and specially intervened in nature to create each human soul.[29] This allowed the position that evolution applied only to the human body, thus preserving human dignity.

The second, and by far the most important, theological objection to evolution is the doctrine of original sin which is based upon a literal, historical approach to Genesis, and the story of Adam and Eve and the serpent. It requires the claim that Adam was an historical person, directly created by God (even if his body evolved from lower forms). As the first human he represented all humanity to God. He was tested and fell, tempted by Satan in the guise of the serpent. And by so doing, he performed an act of disobedience through which the entire human race was condemned not only to physical death, but to death of the soul. The crime was so great that God changed the nature of the world itself, from a paradise where there was no suffering, pain, or death, to the world as we know it. Because of Adam's sin, all humanity is in need of salvation. Original sin *explains* the need for Christ's coming, his death and resurrection. No Adam, no fall; no fall, no atonement; no atonement, no Savior. One can understand why this view of Christianity requires the traditional doctrine of original sin.

The doctrine of original sin insists that the sinful condition of humanity is both an historical and a universal condition, and that humanity is responsible for it. This is the flip side to the positive conviction of the universality of redemption in Christ. The universality of the condition translates into the Church's insistence that all humans came from one couple, and that the condition was transmitted sexually, by generation. Otherwise there might be some humans without original sin, and thus not in need of redemption. When some scientists began to argue that the human species probably developed from earlier species in groups rather than by a single couple (polygenism), the Church condemned such a position, as we saw in Pius XII's *Humani Generis.* Original sin, then, is the sticking point in any Catholic consideration of evolution. To understand the problems with evolution from a Catholic perspective, it is necessary to understand the origin of the doctrine of original sin.

2
Origins of Original Sin

Most of us tend to think that the official Catholic doctrine of original sin has been in the Church right from the start, and is taken from the story of Adam and Eve in Genesis. Actually, it was formulated in a tentative and irregular manner over a period of about four hundred years, standardized finally by that great synthesizer, St. Augustine. Theologians will recognize the particular interpretation of Genesis and the "Fall" in *Catechism* as that of St. Augustine. In the greatest intellectual feat of Christian theology since the letters of St. Paul, Augustine provided the masterful amalgamation of integrated biblical interpretation and neo-Platonic philosophy that has dominated Christianity since his day, and which is still the official teaching of the Catholic Church. It is not true that Augustine invented the concept of original sin, even though the term began with him.[1] It is true that he coordinated and solidified into a smooth story an emerging tradition that, through various formulas, was in the process of formation. How did he arrive at his formulation?

Before going any further, and discussing different people's views of "original sin," we should make clear exactly what we are talking about when we use that term. We should distinguish three ideas, all sometimes referred to as "original sin." First, there is the sin of Adam and Eve, the *peccatum originans*—that is, their specific offense against God that led to their banishment from the garden. Second, there is the state or condition into which all humans are born, which makes them stained or defiled, enemies of God, and condemned to the death of the soul (the *peccatum originatum*). Third, there is "concupiscence," the universal human inclination to sin, a result of the *peccatum originatum*. In current Catholic theology, it is the second item, the state of sin, that is removed by baptism. Concupiscence remains even in the baptized. Many in the Protestant tradition, following Luther, who held that nature was totally corrupted by the fall, equate original sin with concupiscence, an unrestrained drive toward evil. When the traditional Catholic position on original sin is mentioned, it refers to the second idea, the inherited state of sin.

If you ask a Scripture scholar today, most will inform you that there is no "fall," as Augustine describes it, in Genesis.[2] In fact, Adam's story, which some today see as at the heart of the Christian message because it explains why God became human, is hardly mentioned anywhere else in the First Testament. There is hardly any mention of him in the Prophets. What is even more striking is that there is no mention of Adam's sin in the Gospels. As historian of original sin Henri Rondet, S.J. noted, "Obviously the evangelic doctrine of the redemption is not based primarily upon the need to make reparation for Adam's sin. Jesus came 'to seek and to save the lost,' to wrest us away from evil, to restore us to life" (Lk 19:10; Jn 10:10).[3]

It is in Paul that we find the seeds of the Christian doctrine of original sin. In Romans 5:12–21, he draws a parallel between Adam and Christ. Just as Adam brought sin and death into the world, he says, so even more surely Jesus Christ will bring grace and eternal life. Romans 5:19 says, "For just as by the one man's disobedience the many were made sinners, so by the one man's obedience the many will be made righteous." Paul draws conclusions that are not in Genesis, and his exposition is quite brief, but it is clear that he felt that to be human was to be corrupted by sin, and that even creation itself is subject to bondage and decay (Rom 8:19–22).[4]

The Latin translation of Romans 5:12 that was current in the Church for more than a thousand years was faulty, and this may have made it easier for some Church Fathers to assimilate Paul's conclusions and move toward the later concept of original sin. It stated, "Through one man sin entered into the world and through sin death, and thus death has passed unto all men in whom all have sinned." The Latin "in quo," "in whom," is a mistranslation of the Greek "Eph' hō," which means "since" or "because," so that Paul's phrase "in whom all have sinned" should have read "because all have sinned."[5] It was Romans 5:12 that Augustine quoted over and over in his arguments to support the concept of original sin. One should not make too much of this error, however, since Romans 5:19 still says that "by one man's disobedience the many were made sinners," which was Augustine's point.

In the first centuries, redemption was the fundamental assertion, rather than original sin. Clement of Rome (c. A.D. 96), Ignatius of Antioch (A.D. 35–107), and Barnabas (c. A.D. 70) lay stress on the redemption. In their writings we find different points of emphasis.

> And thus they made it manifest that redemption should flow through the blood of the Lord to all them that believe and hope in God. (Clement)[6]

> He loved us when He gave Himself a ransom for us, that He might cleanse us by His blood from our old ungodliness, and bestow life on us when we were almost on the point of perishing through the depravity that was in us. (Ignatius)[7]

> For to this end the Lord endured to deliver up His flesh to corruption, that we might be sanctified through the remission

of sins, which is affected by His blood of sprinkling.
(Barnabas)[8]

The view of Justin (A.D. 100–165) on salvation had little place
for original sin. He and Tatian (~A.D. 160) blamed the devils
for much of humanity's ills. Justin appeared to approve of the
view that demons, who were the offspring of fallen angels and
the daughters of humans, attacked people's souls and bodies,
filling them with vice and corruption. Since Adam and Eve
yielded to the temptation of the Devil, their sin is the prototype of ours.

> He became man by the Virgin, in order that the disobedience
> which proceeded from the serpent might receive its destruc-
> tion in the same manner in which it derived its origin. (Justin)[9]

Tatian, a student of Justin, attacked Greek culture, claiming
that it was a mass of evil compared to the divine purity of
Christianity. He envisioned devils corrupting humans by
teaching them astrology. It was the fallen angels who were
ultimately responsible for the human condition.

> And when men attached themselves to one who was more
> subtle than the rest, having regard to his being the first born,
> and declared him to be God, though he was resisting the law
> of God, then the power of the Logos excluded the beginner of
> the folly and his adherents from all fellowship with Himself.
> And so he who was made in the likeness of God, since the
> more powerful spirit is separated from him, becomes mortal.
> (Tatian)[10]

Demonology was very important in the second century; it was
seen as a kind of answer to the problem of evil or the disorders
of paganism.[11] These early Apologists recognized that our first
parents had free will. If they had been obedient, some
thought they would have attained immortality. For an early

bishop, Theophilus of Antioch (late second century), it is Satan who is the ultimate culprit, not Adam.

> When, then, Satan saw Adam and his wife not only still living, but also begetting children—being carried away with spite because he had not succeeded in putting them to death—when he saw that Abel was well-pleasing to God, he wrought upon the heart of his brother called Cain, and caused him to kill his brother Abel. And thus did death get a beginning in this world, to find its way into every race of man, even to this day.[12]

Irenaeus (A.D. 130–200), bishop of Lyons, argued against Gnostic heresies that were obsessed with trying to explain evil. Irenaeus agreed that Adam's sin dragged humanity into death, but for him, "The history of man is not that of a laborious ascent after a vertical fall, but a providential progress towards a future that is full of promise."[13]

> By this arrangement, therefore, and these harmonies, and a sequence of this nature, man, a created and organized being, is rendered after the image and likeness of the uncreated God— the Father planning everything well and giving His commands, the Son carrying these into execution and performing the work of creating, and the Spirit nourishing and increasing [what is made], but man making progress day by day, and ascending toward the perfect, that is, approximating to the uncreated One. For the Uncreated is perfect, that is, God. Now it was necessary that man should in the first instance be created; and having been created, should receive growth; and having received growth, should be strengthened; and having been strengthened, should abound; and having abounded, should recover [from the disease of sin]; and having recovered, should be glorified; and being glorified, should see his Lord.[14]

Humanity is seen as bound more closely to Christ the second Adam than to the first Adam and his sin.[15] Irenaeus emphasizes the goodness of God who, he says, created humans to have someone on whom to shower his gifts.

Tertullian (A.D. 160–225), a lawyer by training, moved from paganism to orthodoxy to heresy. It was during his orthodox period, however, that he argued that the soul is corporeal, some kind of substance.[16] Therefore, he proposed, we are all linked to Adam because all souls were first of all contained in his and passed on by generation.

> Every soul, then, by reason of its birth, has its nature in Adam until it is born again in Christ; moreover, it is unclean all the while that it remains without this regeneration; and because unclean, it is actively sinful, and suffuses even the flesh (by reason of their conjunction) with its own shame.[17]

This idea, called "traducianism," influenced Augustine, who insisted that Adam's sin was passed to all his descendants by "generation," that is, through the sexual act of procreation. While Augustine held to "generation," he never was able to decide if the soul itself came from Adam's soul, as Tertullian proposed, or if the soul was created directly by God.

However, for Tertullian, this uncleanliness that was passed from generation to generation was thought to be like an evil second nature, something similar to concupiscence, a tendency toward sin, rather than a state of sin that would make us sharers in Adam's guilt.[18] That Tertullian did not hold for an inherited state that would result in damnation without baptism is indicated by his arguments for delay of infant baptism because, he says, infants are going to sin, and true penitence is difficult.[19]

The Greek Father Origen (A.D. 185–254) was an Alexandrian biblical critic, theologian and spiritual writer. While he taught that humans entered the world with a defilement that must be cleansed, he was not too clear about how this happened.

It is written that when Adam had sinned, the Lord banished him from the paradise of delights and that this was the punishment for his sin which, without any possible doubt, passed on to all men. All, in fact, have been sent into this place of humiliation, into this vale of tears, whether all the sons of Adam were in his loins and were expelled with him from paradise, or whether each one of us was banished personally and received his condemnation in some way that we cannot tell and that God only knows.[20]

Origen came to the conclusion, from consideration of the Church's practice of infant baptism and reflection on the rights of purification in the Hebrew Scriptures, that all members of the human race are born with a stain that required cleansing.[21]

Origen was also influenced by the allegorical interpretation of Genesis by Philo (20 B.C.–A.D. 50). Philo, an Alexandrian Jew and a contemporary of Jesus, was concerned with the Jewish faith in the light of Greek philosophy. He considered Adam as an exceptional creature with great powers, a prototype whose descendants are but pale copies. His views, probably based upon rabbinical speculations, influenced Augustine concerning the primitive state of humanity.[22]

Then we have three great theologians, known from their birthplace in Turkey as the Cappadocian Fathers. Original sin was not central for them but was admitted; they stressed the redemption, rejecting much of Origenism and Philo. The statements of Basil, bishop of Caesarea (A.D. 330–379), on Adam's sinning are somewhat ambiguous and difficult to interpret. But he does acknowledge that humanity is fallen.

Basil's brother, Gregory of Nyssa (A.D. 330–395), taught that God created humanity all at once in Adam.[23] Gregory says that to understand man's primitive state we need to understand the resurrection. The resurrection of the body is a return to paradise, where we shall live like the angels without food or sex.[24] The third Cappadocian, Gregory of Nazianzus (A.D. 329–389), like the others, recognizes that we died in Adam, but he says little about the effects of original sin. Instead, he emphasizes the work of Christ in bringing about our salvation.

> This is our present Festival; it is this which we are celebrating today, the Coming of God to Man, that we might go forth, or rather (for this is the more proper expression) that we might go back to God—that putting off the old man, we might put on the New; and that as we died in Adam, so we might live in Christ, being born with Christ and crucified with Him and buried with Him and rising with Him.[25]

John Chrysostom (A.D. 347–407), bishop of Constantinople, the most influential of the Greek Fathers, apparently denied the transmission of original sin. In his homily on Romans, he emphasized, with St. Paul, that Adam was a prototype of Christ. Humans owe their subjection to death to Adam's fault, yet they have been justified and owe their righteousness to Christ. But, he says, the statement that many were made sinners means that Adam's heirs became mortal.

> What then does the word "sinners" mean here? To me it seems to mean liable to punishment and condemned to death. Now that by Adam's death we all became mortals, he had shown clearly and at large.[26]

It is worth noting that the Greek Orthodox church never accepted Augustine's concept of original sin. For them, Adam's sin brought physical death, corruption and mortality, but not a guilt passed on by sexual generation.[27]

Augustine's mentor, Ambrose (A.D. 339–397), witnessed to the presence of original sin in all humanity, and may have had the greatest influence on Augustine.

> For, as we read, Christ "is come to save that which is lost," and "to be Lord both of the dead and the living." In Adam I fell,

in Adam I was cast out of paradise, in Adam I died; how shall
the Lord call me back, except He find me in Adam; guilty as I
was in him, so now justified in Christ.[28]

However, Ambrose appears to connect removal of inherited
sin with the washing of feet rather than with baptism.

Peter was clean, but he must wash his feet, for he had sin by
succession from the first man, when the serpent overthrew
him and persuaded him to sin. His feet were therefore washed,
that hereditary sins might be done away, for our own sins are
remitted through baptism.[29]

It is not clear, however, exactly what Ambrose meant by
hereditary sin. Scholars differ in their assessment of his writings. The patristics scholar Henri Rondet was convinced,
based on the passages quoted above, that Ambrose held a
doctrine of original sin in which all humanity is held guilty
and subject to punishment along with our first parents.
Another distinguished patristics scholar, J. N. D. Kelly, notes
that in other places Ambrose says that we humans shall only
be punished for our personal sins, and not for Adam's.[30]

We should not be surprised that the theology of the early
Fathers is varied and not totally in accord with current orthodoxy. Our familiar creeds had not yet been worked out. Many
of the Fathers were bishops, and they wrote to defend the faith
from concepts foreign to the Scriptures: Gnostics with their
pre-existent souls, Manichees with their evil counterpart to
God, Stoic concepts and Platonic ones. Their reflections were
influenced by the developing Christological doctrines, by the
Church's very early confession of the virgin birth, and by the
liturgical practice of infant baptism. A Christ who possessed the
divine nature must be without sin. This contention was linked
in speculations with the story of the virgin birth and its absence
of sexual generation and the passing along of any stain from
Adam's sin. A second factor was the liturgical practice of infant

baptism, which existed long before any unified concept of original sin had been worked out, and which therefore needed a rationale.[31] While they pondered the Adam and Eve story in Genesis, admitting its pertinence for a description of the true state of humanity, mortal and prone to sin, they did not dwell on it, concentrating on preaching the good news of redemption through the teaching, death and resurrection of Jesus Christ. They emphasized the goal at the end of the race, immortality and union with God.[32]

Augustine and Original Sin

This brings us to Augustine himself (A.D. 354–430), arguably the most influential theologian that Christianity has ever known. Raised by a Christian mother, trained in rhetoric and student of the Latin writers, Augustine has become known for many things—the excesses of his youth, his period as a Manichean, his conversion first to philosophy, and then his conversion and confession to Christ.[33] Augustine was a sensitive individual, troubled with the evils of the world, which he found difficult to reconcile with the good God taught by his mother. He was drawn to the sect of the Manicheans who explained the presence of evil in the world by their doctrine of two supreme powers in the universe, one good and one evil. Convinced by the neo-Platonists that there could be only one God, and that God was good, he left the Manicheans and sought the good life he believed could be grasped by philosophy. But his experience with sin and evil led him to conclude that humans could not do the good without the grace of God, and he eventually converted to Christianity. The realization of the absolute necessity of divine grace for all humans was his greatest achievement, and led to his opposition of Pelagius and his followers, who argued that humans could do good by their own efforts. He was still fighting this battle at his death at age seventy-six.[34]

As a Christian, Augustine's attention shifted from philosophy to Scripture. In his day, Christianity was presented to the educated as a form of "True Wisdom." The Christ of popular imagination was not a suffering savior. There were no crucifixes in the fourth century.[35] Augustine saw Scripture as a mysterious puzzle holding all truth, but it had to be studied and wrestled with prayerfully if God was to reveal its secrets. Once he became a bishop he took the study and expounding of Scripture as his primary task. In the latter years of his life these studies produced three of his greatest works, *On the Trinity*, *The Literal Meaning of Genesis*, and *The City of God*. The first two were written over roughly the same period (c. A.D. 400–416). The third followed from 413 to 426. From about 421 until his death in 430, Augustine also spent increasing amounts of his energy on books written against the disciple of Pelagius, Julian of Eclanum. These were incomplete at his death. It is in these mature works, especially in *The City of God*, that we find Augustine's fully worked out understanding of the divine plan revealed in Scripture.

The "city of God" is contrasted with the "earthly city"—the first oriented to God, the second to self. The story starts with the angels, some of whom sinned and were cast down into hell. This was the foundation of the two cities. Humans, through one man, were created to take the place of the fallen angels, and, if they did not sin, would be granted immortality.

> Man, on the other hand, whose nature was to be a mean between the angelic and the bestial, He created in such a sort, that if he remained in subjection to his creator as his rightful Lord, and piously kept His commandments, he would pass into the company of the angels, and obtain, without the intervention of death, a blessed and endless immortality; but if he offended the Lord his God by a proud and disobedient use of his free will, he should become subject to death, and live as the beasts do—the slave of appetite, and doomed to eternal punishment after death.[36]

Sufficient humans were to be saved to make up for the number of fallen angels; the rest, a majority in Augustine's view, were to be damned.[37] Those to be saved were pre-destined by God according to a mysterious divine choice. Others were pre-destined to eternal death.[38]

God placed Adam in a garden, as Genesis says, and fashioned him a helpmate, Eve, from his rib. They were free from all pain and death, Augustine tells us, and their bodies were under complete control of their intellects. God then allowed the fallen angel, Satan, to enter the serpent and to tempt them to disobedience of God's commands. They exercised their free will in a sin of pride against God. As punishment, they were expelled from the garden of paradise, having merited for themselves and their posterity sin and death, both the physical death in which the soul leaves the body, and the second death when God deserts the soul. In this second state humans would spend eternity in suffering.[39] The condemnation of the human race as the result of Adam's sin is clear in Augustine's presentation.

> For God, the author of natures, not of vices, created man upright; but man, being of his own will corrupted, and justly condemned, begot corrupted and condemned children. For we all were in that one man, since we all were that one man, who fell into sin by the woman who was made from him before the sin. For not yet was the particular form created and distributed to us, in which we as individuals were to live, but already the seminal nature was there from which we were to be propagated; and this being vitiated by sin, and bound by the chain of death, and justly condemned, man could not be born of man in any other state. And thus, from the bad use of free will, there originated the whole train of evil, which, with its concatenation of miseries, convoys the human race from its depraved origin, as from a corrupt root, on to the destruction of the second death, which has no end, those only being excepted who are freed by the grace of God.[40]

In addition to transmitting the condition or state that condemned their descendants to earthly and spiritual death, the very nature of our first parents and their offspring was changed.

> For, as soon as our first parents had transgressed the commandment, divine grace forsook them...and therefore they took fig-leaves...and covered their shame; for though their members remained the same, they had shame now where they had none before. They experienced a new motion of their flesh, which had become disobedient to them, in strict retribution of their own disobedience to God. For the soul, reveling in its own liberty, and scorning to serve God, was itself deprived of the command it had formerly maintained over the body....Then began the flesh to lust against the Spirit, in which strife we are born, deriving from the first transgression a seed of death, and bearing in our members, and in our vitiated nature, the contest or even victory of the flesh.[41]

It is quite clear that Augustine did not confuse the state of original sin, as condemnation to eternal punishment for Adam's descendants, with concupiscence, the tendency to sin or inclination to evil that they also inherited and that for him was typified by sexual lust. Had Adam and Eve not sinned, said Augustine, there would still have been sex in paradise, since humans were made to procreate. But there would have been no sexual excitement in procreating, no "movement of the members" that was not the result of a conscious act of the will.

> At that time, also, a husband would have cleaved to his wife to beget offspring. They would not have had the activity of turbulent lust in their flesh, however, but only the movement of peaceful will by which we command the other members of the body.[42]

The concept that the natural action of human sexual hormones is a divine punishment for Adam's sin has had profound influences on later Christianity. It is responsible for the teaching that sex for pleasure, even in marriage, is somewhat sinful, a view that endured up until modern times.[43] It is also one of the concepts that supported the idea that celibacy is a higher, more spiritual state than marriage.

Throughout these later works of Augustine human suffering and death are presented as punishments for Adam's sin.[44] Even further, because of Adam's sin "All nature was changed for the worst."[45] The very nature of nature was changed. The natural evils of sickness, storms, earthquakes, wild animals, and unforeseen accidents are all part of the punishment administered by a just and righteous God.[46]

These then are the concepts in Augustine's story of the origins and state of the human race. We should observe the logic Augustine followed to put the story together. It hinges on his struggle with the problem of evil. Augustine the Christian had been convinced of several things concerning the divine nature. From his experience with the Manicheans and the neo-Platonists he had concluded that there was no evil principle in the world matching that of the good God. The all-powerful God, creator of all things, was totally good, and because God was omnipotent nothing could happen without the divine approval. Yet, Augustine was fully conscious that the world was filled not only with evil people, but with natural evil of staggering proportions. In particular he noted many times the suffering of innocent babies who could not have committed any wrong by their own wills. How was he to reconcile the pain and suffering in the world with an all-powerful, all-good God?

First, he concluded that evil was due to evil wills, the wrong use by humanity of their free will. Second, evil spirits, the fallen angels, were allowed by God to torment humanity, a powerful conviction of his time.[47] Third, since God was omnipotent, evil could not occur unless God permitted it. What possible circumstance could result in the all-good God allowing such evil, particularly in cases where innocents were tormented? There needed to be another powerful cause. Augustine found his cause in his scriptural story of the creation and fall of the human race. The cause was Adam's sin, the sin of the whole race, a crime against God so vast and horrible that justice demanded terrible punishment be inflected on the whole human race. Only by making God directly responsible for natural evil could Augustine continue to hold that this God was all-powerful. Because he also held that God was good, he had to balance this by insisting that punishment was necessary because God was all-just. His concept of justice overwhelmed his understanding of God as love. Augustine berates Julian of Eclanum, Pelagius' pupil, for not admitting that Adam's sin demanded the infliction of the world's evils.

> You do not wish to say from the beginning, when the human race deserted God, it contracts the offense of its condemned origin, which fully deserves to suffer all these punishments it endures except where the inscrutable wisdom of the Creator spares it, mysteriously, according to His plan.[48]

When Julian pointed to the injustice of punishing innocents with damnation if they died without baptism, Augustine revealed his vision of the cold and awful majesty of God demanded by his interpretation of Scripture.

> Who are we to ask God why He condemns the one instead of the other? Shall the object molded say to him who molded it: "Why hast thou made me thus?" Is not the potter master of his clay, to make from the same mass of vitiated and condemned origin one vessel for honorable use according to mercy, and another for dishonorable use according to justice?[49]

Concerning the baptism of infants, Augustine argued that the fact that the Church had always done this proved that the terrible sin at the beginning of the race indeed had occurred, and that it had been passed along to them by generation.[50]

Augustine's views on original sin have held sway even to

today. They have come down to us through the Council of Carthage (A.D. 418), which condemned Pelagius; through the Second Council of Orange (A.D. 529) approved by Pope Boniface II, which condemned the Semi-Pelagians, and finally through the Council of Trent (A.D. 1546).

The two key statements of Carthage were as follows.

> Whoever says that Adam, the first man, was made mortal in the sense that he was to die a bodily death whether he sinned or not, which means that to quit the body would not be a punishment for sin but a necessity of nature, *anathema sit*.

> If anyone denies that infants newly born from their mother's womb are to be baptized, even when born from baptized parents; or says that, though they are baptized for the remission of sins, yet they do not contract from Adam any trace of original sin which must be expiated by the bath of regeneration that leads to eternal life, so that in their case the formula of baptism "for the forgiveness of sins" would no longer be true but would be false, *anathema sit*.[51]

Additional canons insisted on the necessity of grace to avoid sin and to perform the divine commands.

The Canons of Orange on original sin repeated and strengthened those of Carthage. Taking their material from the writings of Augustine, the document asserts:

> If anyone says that the whole person, that is, in both body and soul, was not changed for the worse through the offense of Adam's transgression, but that only the body became subject to corruption with the liberty of the soul remaining unharmed, then he has been deceived by Pelagius' error and opposes the Scripture which says, "The soul which sins shall die" [Ez 18:20] and "Do you not know that if you show yourselves ready to obey anyone, you are the slaves of the one you obey?" [Rom 6:16] and "A person is judged the slave of the one who conquers him" [2 Pt 2:19].

> If anyone asserts that the transgression of Adam harmed him alone and not his progeny, or that the damage is only by the death of the body which is a punishment for sin, and thus does not confess that the sin itself which is the death of the soul also passed through one person into the whole human race, then he does injustice to God, contradicting the Apostle who says, "Through one person sin entered the world and through sin death, and thus it passed to all humans, in whom all have sinned" [Rom 5:12].[52]

Orange affirmed Augustine's theology of grace, stating that grace is required for both faith and good works, but denied his position that souls were predestined to hell. Augustine's view of original sin was now the official position of the Church.

From Augustine to Trent

Most of the great medieval churchmen were disciples of Augustine in the matter of original sin. It was necessary to wait until Anselm of Canterbury (A.D. 1033–1109) for something significantly new on the subject to be proposed. Anselm argued that one could understand the necessity of the Incarnation by considering the human situation as recorded in Genesis.[53] His argument went like this. God made humanity for happiness and to enjoy God. Humanity sinned and ruined God's plan. Sin robs God of his honor. Humanity cannot be saved unless satisfaction is made for God's honor, a satisfaction that is proportional to guilt. But humanity cannot pay the debt because they owe everything to God. Humanity cannot pay the debt, and God, in justice, ought not to, so it is necessary for Christ to save humanity, or God's plan would not be accomplished and that is impossible.

This formed the basis for Anselm's later reflections on the virginal conception and original sin, where his unique negative

definition of original sin appears.[54] Original sin is the depriva-
tion or absence of justice. Humans should possess justice, a rec-
titude of the will, a will in conformity with God's will, and due
to Adam's sin, they do not. Adam's sin changed human nature.
In Adam's case the person tainted our nature; in our case, our
nature taints the person.

> Thus in Adam the person despoiled the nature of the good of
> justice, and the nature, once impoverished, makes every per-
> son it engenders from itself sinful and unjust, by virtue of that
> same poverty. In this way the personal sin of Adam passes over
> into all who are naturally propagated from him, and becomes
> original or natural in them.[55]

Anselm's redefinition of original sin as an absence or depriva-
tion has continued to be an active part of original sin speculation, as we shall see, even to the present.

Thomas Aquinas (A.D. 1225–1274) accepted Anselm's
view that original sin is a privation, and he expanded it.
Thomas saw our first parents created by God in a state of original justice which included sanctifying grace and infused
virtues. Humanity was elevated above its nature into a state of
harmony between soul and body. In this state they were
immortal, enlightened and preserved from injury and pain.
Through a sin of pride, they were deprived of original justice
and grace, and left to their nature.[56]

Adam's sin was a sin of human nature, and all humanity is
in him. And Thomas repeated Anselm's thought.

> Original sin spread in this way, that at first the person infected
> the nature, and afterwards the nature infected the person.[57]

Original sin is spread by generation, going with human
nature, even though souls are directly created by God.
Original sin is a disorder, an absence of harmony and a spiritual illness. The real character of original sin is the privation of

original justice. Its effect on the soul is concupiscence. The body and its appetites are no longer under control of the soul.

While both Augustine and Anselm had relegated infants born with original sin to damnation of the mildest degree, Thomas concluded that such infants would be denied the vision of God but would not suffer.

The next noteworthy step in this overview of original sin occurs with Martin Luther and the Reformation. Luther concluded that, as a result of Adam's sin, human nature became totally depraved and humans lost their free will.

> So, if we believe that Satan is the prince of this world...and that he does not let his prisoners go unless he is driven out by the power of the Divine Spirit, it is again apparent that there can be no "free-will."...So if we believe that original sin has ruined us to such an extent that even in the godly, who are led by the Spirit, it causes abundance of trouble by striving against good, it is clear that in a man who lacks the Spirit nothing is left that can turn itself to good, but only to evil.[58]

Luther related the depths of corruption to which humanity had fallen by original sin to concupiscence.

> What then is original sin?...According to the subtleties of the theologians, it is the privation of original justice. But according to the Apostle and in the simple words of Jesus Christ, it is not merely the privation of a quality in the will, nor of light in the intelligence, nor of vigor in the memory, but a privation of all integrity in all the powers, both of body and soul, in the whole man, interior and exterior. It is the readiness to do evil, the repugnance for good, the distaste for light and wisdom, the love or error and darkness, the avoidance of and supreme contempt for good works, the unrestrained drive for evil. The holy Fathers have said that original sin is concupiscence, the law of the flesh, the law of the members, a weakness of nature, a tyrant, a congenital illness.[59]

Luther called on Augustine for support of his position that humanity had totally lost its free will, but it seems that in this matter he misread Augustine. Augustine struggled all his life with the relationship between God's grace and free will. He maintained the necessity for both throughout his life, from his early book arguing for free will to his later works against the Pelagians. Late in life, Augustine wrote:

> It is not, therefore, true, as some affirm that we say, and as that correspondent of yours ventures moreover to write, that "all are forced into sin," as if they were unwilling, "by the necessity of their flesh"; but if they are already of the age to use the choice of their own mind, they are both retained in sin by their own will, and by their own will are hurried along from sin to sin.[60]

As can be seen in the following excerpt, Calvin followed Luther in his view of total depravity.

> But to sin in this case, is to become corrupt and vicious; for the natural depravity which we bring from our mother's womb, though it bring not forth immediately its own fruits, is yet sin before God, and deserves his vengeance: and this is that sin which they call original. For as Adam at his creation had received for us as well as for himself the gifts of God's favor, so by falling away from the Lord, he in himself corrupted, vitiated, depraved, and ruined our nature; for having been divested of God's likeness, he could not have generated seed but what was like himself.[61]

For the Reformers, original sin is not removed by baptism; rather baptism is a sign that complete remission has been made for this sin by Christ, both of the guilt that should have been imputed to us, and the punishment that we all deserve. To be justified means to no longer be held responsible for this state of sin. However, this sin, this concupiscence, remains, and must be struggled against throughout life. However, babies who die without baptism are not condemned to eternal death, according to Calvin; they are saved by Christ's special love for them.[62]

This brings us to the Council of Trent, which reacted against Luther's view that, because of Adam's sin, human nature became totally depraved, by looking back to the thought of Augustine as canonized by the Council of Carthage. In indicating that the human will could still resist evil if helped by God's grace, the Council fathers were afraid they might be charged with Pelagian views, so they repeated the anti-Pelagian positions of Augustine in their official statements.

In summary, the Council of Trent said the following:

1) Adam sinned, lost original holiness, incurred the wrath of God, incurred death, and slavery under the power of the devil, and was changed to a worse state.

2) Adam lost righteousness and holiness for his descendants, transmitting the sin which is the death of the soul, as well as bodily death and pains.

3) Adam's sin, transmitted by propagation, is present in all humans and is removed only by the merit of Christ. This merit is applied to infants and adults in baptism. Christ reconciled us with God by his blood.

4) Infants must be baptized to be cleansed from original sin so that they may enter the kingdom of God.

5) By baptism the offense of original sin is truly taken away, not covered. Concupiscence remains in the baptized. This can be resisted through the grace of Christ.

These, then, are the solemn decisions on original sin in Catholic teaching.[63] They form the basis of the teaching as presented in the new Catechism.

Conclusion

Since the doctrine of original sin held by the church is essentially derived from St. Augustine, it is essential to know the historical background for his views and to examine his logic in developing it. It was found to be based on the literal interpretation of Genesis, with Adam and Eve as historical personages, and also based upon Augustine's philosophical struggle with the nature of evil. Augustine then fit his conclusions into his elaborate picture of the creation and destiny of the human race. The history of original sin since Augustine revealed that the Council of Trent, when it had to take a stand, returned to his views on original sin.

Augustine's picture of "what really happened" includes the idea that the world was once a paradise without death or suffering. Human beings began their existence perfected far above our present condition and have degenerated. Human nature, and the nature of nature itself, was changed at a point in time for the worse. Obviously such ideas are at variance with the findings and theories of modern science. We can conclude either that the scientific data and the theories built upon it are going to be proven wrong, or that the Church needs to revise its traditional and official interpretation of Scripture and revealed truth in this case. To put it simply, since there can be only one truth, one vision of human origins is mistaken. We shall consider both of these possibilities in later chapters.

3
Post-Vatican II Advances

The best-kept secret of Vatican II concerns the nature of revelation. Students of ecumenical councils know that the statements they produce are driven by the particular theological controversies faced at the time, and that the wording of the documents issued is the result of careful compromise. The documents of Vatican II were massaged until they received almost unanimous agreement from the prelates present. Because of the compromise nature of such documents, they often require careful study and interpretation to uncover their significant features. A good example of this process is Vatican II's *Dogmatic Constitution on Divine Revelation (Dei verbum)*.

Ecclesiologist Gregory Baum has done a study of the four revisions to the document worked out over a three year period.[1] He notes that the original draft prepared by Cardinal Ottaviani saw revelation essentially as doctrine, with Scripture and tradition as the two sources of that doctrine. Truths were claimed for tradition that were not in Scripture, while Scripture was claimed to be totally inerrant and historically accurate. The Church's magisterium was declared the "proximate norm of belief," and theology's job was to harmonize Scripture with what the Church teaches. The Council Fathers protested against this presentation, and Pope John XXIII sent

the whole package off to be revised, after adding Cardinal
Bea's Secretariat for Christian Unity to the drafting team.

As early as the second draft, Baum tells us, words were
included which distinguished God's self-revelation in word
and action in Israel from the Spirit-inspired record of these
events in Scripture. A turning point had been reached.[2] In the
final version, revelation is primarily the self-disclosure of God
in history in view of humanity's salvation. The "two-source"
theory is removed. Scripture and tradition become the *means
of transmission* of revelation. The material sufficiency of
Scripture—the idea that all truth necessary for salvation is
contained in Scripture—is left open for ecumenical reasons,
and literary criticism of Scripture is approved. On the
inerrancy of Scripture, the guarantee of truth contained in it is
stated to pertain to those things necessary for our salvation.
The idea that the main task of theology is to justify the teaching of the magisterium disappears.

There are statements referring to other models of revelation in *Dei verbum,* but the attentive reader will note that
Chapter 1 is entitled "Divine Revelation Itself," and states
that what God reveals is the divine self. Chapter 2, "The
Transmission of Divine Revelation," describes Scripture
and tradition as the means through which this revelation
takes place. The key point here is that, technically, revelation is an experience of interpersonal communion with the
self-revealing God, responded to with faith. The Bible is
not revelation. Doctrines are not revelation. Scripture and
tradition are witnesses to revelation. They are the human
product of divinely inspired encounters with selected members of the human community. This point is important for
the proper understanding of Church teaching.

The Council's teaching on revelation has been the subject of
a recent study by fundamental theologian Gerald O'Collins,
S.J. He is concerned that these concepts have been ignored.
"Even *Dei verbum* has not been properly received," he notes,

"and, in many quarters, now tends to be half-forgotten."[3] O'Collins presents a bibliography of documents studying *Dei verbum*, and summarizes their results.

> The secondary literature has singled out various other merits and achievements of *Dei verbum:* the way in which the presentation of revelation as primarily an encounter with the self-disclosing God puts into a new context the whole debate about the relationship between tradition and sacred scripture; the emphasis on the unity between tradition and scripture in the transmission and reactualization of revelation; the endorsement of scientific biblical scholarship; the interpretation of biblical truth as salvific; the stress on the role of scripture for theology; and the stimulus given to the use of the Bible in every area of the church's life.[4]

While it would be a gross error to identify revelation with the Scriptures, there certainly is a revelatory content contained in them. It is appropriate to refer to them as "the word of God" because they were inspired by the Holy Spirit. Yet, not everything contained in Scripture is revelation. As O'Collins tells us, "The mere fact that the inspiration of the Holy Spirit operated in the writing of these books is no necessary and immediate gauge of the 'amount' of divine self-revelation to which they witness."[5] The primary revelatory content in Scripture is that God is love and has sent his Son, Jesus Christ, for our salvation. This revelation in Christ is definitive and unrepeatable; O'Collins prefers to refer to it as "foundational." But, since revelation is the encounter experience, though its content is complete in the Christ event, revelation itself is a present reality. We experience revelation today primarily in the liturgy, in the reading of the word, and participation in the sacraments. We also experience it in interaction with the Spirit of Christ present in each other. O'Collins calls the individual's experience of revelation "dependent." Non-experienced revelation would be a contradiction in terms.

O'Collins points out that post-conciliar theology is developing an approach to revelation as God's symbolic self-communication. All experience is symbolic. Sights and sounds act as signs and symbols to disclose and communicate the divine mystery. There seems to be a growing consensus among theologians since Vatican II that revelation is best spoken of as "symbolic mediation."[6] The apostles and the other authors of Scripture interpreted their experiences of the early Christian community and were inspired to write down what they did.

Concerning revelatory symbols, O'Collins notes that other Vatican II documents speak of liturgical signs and symbols that mediate Christ's self-communication. But revelation is offered to all people, and even the signs of the times, we are told, may reveal where and how God is working in the world.[7] It is the task of pastors and theologians to discern these signs. One such sign of our times that we wish to call attention to, and will reflect upon later, is the scientific realization that the whole universe, including human beings, has evolved. What is the revealed content in this recognition?

Catholic Biblical Scholarship and Interpretation of Genesis

Catholic biblical scholarship took a major step forward in 1943 when Pope Pius XII in his encyclical *Divino Afflante Spiritu* encouraged the use of modern scientific methods in studying the Bible. Vatican II's *Dei verbum* strongly approved use of the historical-critical method of biblical analysis, which attempts to establish what the biblical authors intended to convey in their texts. The encyclical states:

> Those who search out the intention of the sacred writers must, among other things, have regard for "literary forms." For truth is proposed and expressed in a variety of ways, depending on whether a text is history of one kind or another, or

whether its form is that of prophecy, poetry, or some other type of speech. The interpreter must investigate what meaning the sacred writer intended to express and actually expressed in particular circumstances as he used contemporary literary forms in accordance with the situation of his own time and culture. For the correct understanding of what the sacred author wanted to assert, due attention must be paid to the customary and characteristic styles of perceiving, speaking, and narrating which prevailed at the time of the sacred writer, and to the customs men normally followed at that period in their everyday dealings with one another.[8]

Today, this method involves textual criticism of the ancient manuscripts; linguistic and semantic analysis, using the knowledge of historical philology; literary criticism to determine the textual units; genre criticism of the times and their histories; tradition criticism; and finally redaction criticism which studies the modifications the texts have undergone before reaching their final state. *Dei verbum* also urged that the text be read and interpreted "according to the same Spirit by whom it was written" and with regard for the content and unity of the whole of Scripture.

Upon reflection, it is easy to see how Vatican II's emphasis on Scripture as the means for the transmission of divine revelation forms a logical basis for the methods of Scripture interpretation also endorsed by the Council. For if God uses human beings as channels through which to make divine purposes known, this means that revelation comes to us cloaked in the symbols of human experience, conformed to the limitations of human language, and shaped by human knowledge of the world. Therefore, what the authors of Scripture were inspired to write were human stories, histories, poetry and prose, sagas, legends, myths and laws, which contain that which God wishes them to contain for the purpose of our salvation. We recognize these words as the Word of God because, when they are read in faith, we experience the divine presence revealing itself to us in ways that we can understand.

The extent of our understanding of the revealed content of Scripture is limited by our understanding of the human writing in which it is transmitted. We need to understand the meaning of the words, the idioms used during the eras of the writers, the customs of the people, the level of scientific knowledge they had, and the current myths and stories used in their time to explain the world in which they lived. Without these things we can still understand something of Scripture, but we are severely handicapped and open to misunderstandings, often deceived into thinking that the books provide ready answers to all the problems of life.

The books of Scripture are the Church's books too; they were formed in the community of believers and are best read and understood in the community of believers, read in the same Spirit by which they were formed, read as part of the whole understanding of the Church. Each part needs to be tested and discerned against the totality of the written word, if it is to be properly understood.

What then do the Scripture scholars tell us about the content of divine revelation contained in the first books of Genesis? The first books of Genesis proclaim to all that the universe, and everything in it, is totally dependent upon God. In story and myth, providing imaginative explanations for the causes of the human condition, we hear that we are called to live in a purposefully created universe, as God's faithful people, in accord with divine plans. Humans, made for community, somehow mirror the supreme consciousness, yet are prone to disobedience, and susceptible to temptation, failing without the continued assistance of God. Genesis is a record proclaiming that God never gives up on humanity, continuing to gift it in spite of continuous falls. In theological terms, humanity is not capable of achieving its destiny on its own without the grace of God. Humanity is in need of redemption.[9]

The scholars are even more positive in affirming what the revelatory content of Genesis is not. It is not a lesson in cosmology or biology.[10] It is not an explanation of the origin of evil. Scripture scholar Walter Brueggemann reminds us of this when he writes:

> Frequently, this text is treated as though it were an explanation of *how evil came into the world*. But the Old Testament is never interested in such an abstract issue. In fact, the narrative gives no explanation for evil. There is no hint that the serpent is the embodiment of the principle of evil.[11]

There is no portrayal of a "fall" from immortality. Humanity has not been changed from how it was created. Death, suffering, and work are part of the human destiny, not divine punishment. There is no justification in Genesis for the subjugation of women or for the destruction of the earth's resources for human purposes.[12]

Concerning the particular subject of evolution, scripture scholar Bruce Vawter concludes that Genesis does not deal with the topic.

> The story of the "fall" is a paradigm of human conduct in the face of temptation, not a lesson in biology. We conclude, therefore, that just as it has long been recognized that the imagery of Genesis says nothing either *pro* or *contra* the scientific hypothesis of the evolution of man from lower species, it should be recognized as well that neither does it pronounce anything for or against the hypotheses of single or multiple origins of man's own species.
>
> In sum, the traditional doctrine of original sin is not to be found in Genesis....[13]

This is a far cry from a fundamentalist approach to Genesis 1–3.

The approach of modern Scripture scholars is officially endorsed by the Church hierarchy today. In 1994, the Pontifical Biblical Commission issued The Interpretation of

the Bible in the Church, a significant expansion and extension
of the explanation of biblical interpretation in the Church
endorsed by Vatican II.[14] Use of the historical-critical method
is strongly supported, but, to be supportive of faith, it must
take into account the final results of the editorial process and
interpret the meaning of the texts for today. Thus, the historical *(diachronic)* method can be usefully supplemented by various *synchronic* approaches concerned with the language,
composition, narrative structure and capacity for persuasion of
the final form of the text. A multitude of old and new methods
of interpretation are examined in some detail in this document,
and their advantages and limitations are assessed. These
include rhetorical analysis which looks at the persuasive aspects
of the text; narrative analysis which is attentive to plot, charac-
terization and the narrative world of texts; and semiotic analysis which examines the relationships within the scriptural
language.

Each of these methods has some useful potential, as do the
various approaches based upon tradition, such as interpretation within the light of the canon of Scripture, use of Jewish
traditions of interpretation, and methods that examine the
historical influence of the texts. Approaches that use the
human sciences have also provided some points of enlighten-
ment, as have contextual approaches such as those coming
out of liberation and feminist theology. The document is a
splendid summary of the state of the art, and is recommended
reading for all involved in catechesis, and all seriously inter-
ested in Scripture studies.

We should note, in addition, that the Pontifical Biblical
Commission is completely in tune with Vatican II on the
nature of revelation.

> The Bible...does not present itself as a direct revelation of timeless truths but as the written testimony to a series of interventions in which God reveals himself in human history.[15]

In the light of what we have been saying about revelation and Catholic biblical scholarship, it should come as no surprise that the document contains the strongest repudiation of fundamentalist interpretation issued by the Catholic Church to date.

> The fundamentalist approach is dangerous, for it is attractive to people who look to the Bible for ready answers to the problems of life. It can deceive these people, offering them interpretations that are pious but illusory....Fundamentalism actually invites people to a kind of intellectual suicide. It injects into life a false certitude, for it unwittingly confuses the divine substance of the biblical message with what are in fact its human limitations.[16]

The clear acceptance by the Church of historical-critical methods of biblical interpretation provides strong support for theologians anxious to reexamine doctrines based upon older, more literal, approaches to Scripture.

Theologians on Original Sin and Evolution

Catholic theologians in recent years have worked to update their understanding of original sin, using the fruits of human knowledge in the various secular areas. Less work has been done to explore the implications of an evolutionary worldview.

Theological speculation on original sin since just before Vatican II can be characterized as having five significant features: a Christological orientation, a deconstruction of Trent, the incorporation of psychological and sociological insights, a vision of Genesis 1–11 as the result of an evolutionary process, and a struggle between situationalist and personalist philosophical views concerning original sin as a distinct reality.

We should discuss each of these trends, to grasp what has been going on in original sin studies since the Council. Following this overview, a modern synthesis that contains the best of these developments will be examined.[17]

Christological Orientation

Assuming now the modern biblical studies we discussed earlier in this chapter, this factor is probably the most significant advance in the original sin debate, and is generally shared by all participants. It involves the deep realization that when "original sin" is mentioned, the subject really being debated is our salvation in Jesus Christ as proclaimed in the Scriptures: Scriptures that say almost nothing about "original sin." To begin at the beginning, consider that the first breath of anything like the traditional concept of "original sin" comes in Romans 5:12–21, and even there it is clear to scholars today that Paul's intent was Christological. Paul set up a parallel between Christ the new being and Adam the old. From Adam the first man sin and death came into the world because all have sinned, he said. It is humanity's sins that are being recognized. With Christ comes redemption for all from sin and death. It is universal redemption in Jesus Christ that is being proclaimed.[18]

Theologians such as Karl Rahner and his student Karl Heinz-Weger have stressed that God's grace is present to humanity from the first. There is no initial period of time where alienation from God holds sway without the redeeming presence of Christ; and the grace of Christ, thanks to the divine will for universal salvation, is stronger than any obstacle such as original sin, however it be understood. What this means is that the concept of "original sin" needs to be understood from the perspective of our redemption in Jesus Christ, not the other way around. The Father did not send the Son to patch up some broken divine plan for humanity. God's self-communication in love points us toward the kingdom ahead, not a paradise lost.[19] In Gabriel Daly's summary of the question,

> The core of the doctrine traditionally labeled "original sin" is the assertion that to be human is to need redemption. The bare fact of being a member of the species *Homo sapiens* means that we need reconciling and healing by divine grace even before we have actually done anything sinful. Christians profess that the reconciling and healing is effected by a first-century Jew, Jesus of Nazareth, whose life, death and resurrection constitute a unique manifestation of God's salvific will and power.[20]

Interpretation of Trent

The second significant feature influencing recent studies on original sin is the application of historical-literary criticism to documents of the Church. If it is recognized that Scripture is also human literature and has to be interpreted by historical and literary techniques, how much more so later documents of the Church. Theologians have realized that irreformability of dogmas means that while the meaning of a dogma does not change, the expression of that meaning is culturally conditioned and must be carefully interpreted. In his excellent study of the interpretation of documents of the magisterium, Francis Sullivan, S.J. summarized the situation facing theologians.

> To sum up: a dogma is an ecclesial proposition which expresses some aspect of divine revelation. Its formulation is always historically and culturally conditioned. It is a true statement, but it never says the whole truth, and it may be mixed with elements that are not part of revealed truth....A dogma is not identical with the original word of revelation. The truth of a dogmatic statement is guaranteed by the Spirit, but it is not written under the Spirit's inspiration, as scripture is.[21]

Theologians at Trent, Sullivan also noted, "in their under-standing of original sin, took the story of the fall in chapter 3 of Genesis far more literally than it is appropriate for modern theologians to do."[22]

Trent was answering the Reformers on justification, and in support of that the council fathers needed to correct the Reformer's teaching on the radical corruption of human nature by Adam's sin. Preparation of their decree was rushed (it was prepared and promulgated in three weeks), so they settled for just five canons. One affirmed, against the Reformers, that baptism removed rather than just covered over the guilt due to original sin. Concupiscence, a disordered state of human appetites, was stated to be different from original sin, and to be present even in the baptized. When Catholics argued that human nature was not totally depraved, they were accused of having a Pelagian bias. To make clear that this was not so the Council Fathers "reproduced the basically Augustinian teaching of the Council of Carthage (A.D. 418) and the Second Council of Orange (A.D. 529)."[23] The historical nature of Adam and Eve was not defined when they did this; it was assumed.[24] The same kind of analysis can be applied to other Church pronouncements that touch on the subject, and the crux of the matter is that there are no official church teachings that would prevent the development of the doctrine of original sin in accord with modern knowledge of the world and of the gospel.

Psychological and Sociological Insights

Our third factor affecting current reflections on original sin is the incorporation of modern psychological and sociological insights. The psychological theories of Freud were seen to enlighten the internal conflict in humans that was expressed in the traditional idea of concupiscence. The passions and instincts struggling against the rational desire to do the good has often been noted: by St. Paul and Augustine, for example. Freud's investigation and exposure of the human unconscious, revealing the *id* driven by its "pleasure principle" struggling against the rational *ego*, the dualism of the unconscious versus the conscious, provided psychological insights into the nature of concupiscence. This self-alienation in us is natural, not sin. However, it can lead to sin, or to constructive activities.

Insights from the social sciences have been helpful in consideration of the transmission of original sin, said by Trent to occur by generation, not imitation. But Trent did not discuss the meaning of "generation." For modern theologians it is considered to apply to the whole process of socialization that occurs when humans enter the world and are assimilated into the family, the local community, and the wider social sphere.[25] The principal idea is that humans find themselves thrust into a world where sinful people, activities and structures are already in place, and influencing and training the mind long before it is capable of making fully free moral decisions. We are contaminated by evil just by being born, by our generation into the human race, and not just by imitating our ancestors. Both psychologically and sociologically we absorb the values and convictions of family, community and society at large, long before we are capable of reflecting upon them. Psychologically, in Freudian terms, the *superego* is formed by society in accord with society's values and becomes conscience. Going against this malformed conscience is felt as guilt. No wonder this state has been considered an involuntary defect, an *aversio a Deo,* an aversion to God, sometimes experienced as a demonic bondage of the will. Here we gain some understanding of that solidarity in evil that transcends the sum of individual human sins.[26]

The Evolutionary Viewpoint

The fourth aspect of post-Vatican II theological speculation on original sin is the intervention of an evolutionary viewpoint, released by modern critical understanding of Genesis. The seeds for an evolutionary approach to theology were planted by the Jesuit paleontologist and mystic, Pierre Teilhard de Chardin (1881–1955). Teilhard was the first Catholic churchman to be totally caught up in the concept of evolution. He considered it the key to all human understanding.[27] God can only create by evolution, said Teilhard. And God gains something apparently from the world. The three mysteries of Creation, Incarnation and Redemption are no more than three modes or aspects of the same process, a fourth mystery, the creative union of the whole world in God.[28] Love is the radial energy that is driving the evolution of matter toward spirit, Teilhard said. Christ came to direct and animate the Christian phylum or biological group, the leading shoot of biogenesis, as the universe moves toward its destiny in God-omega, the endpoint of evolution.[29]

Although many Catholics were grasped by Teilhard's vision, he was censured by the Church for his views, and forbidden to publish on theology and evolution. He remained obedient to his superiors; his work was published posthumously. His influence was present at Vatican II, as we noted earlier, and since then has continued, although muted and usually below the surface.[30]

Teilhard had no systematically worked out theory of original sin, although he commented upon it in various of his works.[31] He saw creation by evolution as the act of arrangement and unification of a multiple of creatable forms. He is not clear if there is some element of pre-existence in these forms.[32] The multiple is not sinful, but its gradual unification involves a multitude of tentative probings in space-time that are filled with error and suffering. Statistically, it is inevitable that disorders occur, he said. As the evolved levels reach the level of life, we have suffering, and with humanity it becomes sin. In general, he saw original sin in association with the problem of evil, and as a necessary result of the finite nature of creation and the evolution of free will. As a paleontologist, and familiar with the on-going historical-critical studies of *Genesis*, Teilhard saw the traditional Augustinian interpretation of paradise at the beginning of history as an embarrassment.[33]

While Teilhard did not specifically pursue the subject of original sin, a number of other theologians, realizing that the scientific support for evolution was strong and growing, began to explore how its tenets could be squared with the Church's pronouncements on original sin. Was Adam the first man to reach a self-conscious level? Was there one first human or a group? Paleontologists seemed to believe that the human species arose as a group, a theory called polygenism, rather than as an individual (monogenism). In response, speculations included the idea that Adam meant the first couple, or more likely the group. Or, Adam was seen as the symbol for corporate humanity, and since we are united as a species, and called by God as a species, when one sinned, all were responsible.[34] It was the growth of the newly grasped Christological factor, discussed earlier, that finally put such questions as these to flight for these theologians. The unity of the human race is in our destiny, they concluded, not our beginning. Original sin, as the dark side of our need for salvation, applies to all, because we are all called by God and all redeemed by Jesus Christ. Furthermore, with the acceptance of evolution, and as a result of modern biblical studies, they dropped talk of paradise.

Influenced by the evolutionary ideas of Teilhard de Chardin, several Dutch theologians, in particular Peter Schoonenberg, S.J., and Ansfried Hulsbosch, O.S.A., further pursued the problem of original sin in this new context. Schoonenberg recognized that God created through evolution and that creativity is continuous. Therefore, he said, there is no reason to postulate

the "immediate" creation of the human soul; all creation is
immediate. The ascent toward man in evolution is the ascent
toward God's image.[35] The fall is not due to the sin of Adam
alone, he proposed, it is due to the whole history of sin in the
world.[36] Schoonenberg used the existentialist concept of "being
situated" in the world, in this case, a world that was sinful.
Original sin, then, can be thought of as "the sin of the world," as
mentioned in John 1:29.

Hulsbosch also accepted the concept of human evolution
as the true state of affairs. We must evaluate God's creation
primarily with reference to the end, he said.

> God creates the world and humanity in and unto Christ. For
> us who live in time this work of creation is being consum-
> mated. The intention of God's creation is consummated in the
> course of cosmic evolution. This point of departure governs
> everything in a theology of evolution.[37]

Paradise was not at the beginning, said Hulsbosch, it is at the
end. Under the creative action of God, humanity evolved
from lower forms of life and was made with a desire for God.
But it is impossible for humanity to achieve union with God
without the gift of God's grace. By our human nature we are
related to others in the world, and the world we are born into
is sinful. "Original sin is the powerlessness, arising from
nature, of man in his incompleteness as creature to reach his
freedom and to realize the desire to see God, *insofar* as this
impotence is put into the context of a sinful world."[38] By
accepting the gift of God's grace, says Hulsbosch, we become
a new creature, possessing through the Spirit of Christ a mode
of being to which we are being called. "The man whom God
creates *is man as he shall be at the end.*"[39]

In light of a rather negative theological climate on evolution
at the time, most theologians just before and since Vatican II
have avoided direct studies of the concept itself. An exception
was Karl Rahner. As early as 1958, Rahner wrote a major study

on the subject.[40] He concluded in favor of evolution; that is, he saw it as compatible with Scripture and the Christian message. Concerning the points of objection raised by *Humani generis*, he saw no need to insist on the special creation of the human soul, since God's creative action is continuous and to insist on a special immediate creation of each soul would be to make God a secondary cause, which is theologically unacceptable. It is unacceptable because it reduces God from the ultimate ground of all creation to a secondary role of action within the universe and dependence upon it. Concerning the scientific postulate of polygenism, i.e., a number of humans evolving as a group, which Pius XII saw as inconsistent with the doctrine of original sin since some might not have descended directly from the historical Adam, Rahner first argued against it, but later, changing his mind, found it acceptable. Unity of the human race, he noted, does not depend upon physical descent from one hypothetical person. The race is united as one species, and, more importantly, united in humanity's destiny in Christ.[41]

Original Sin as a Distinct Reality

The fifth feature of post-Vatican II speculation on original sin deserves special attention, as it treats a crucial element of the teaching of Trent, one that especially distinguishes the Catholic view of original sin. We refer to the question: Is original sin a distinct reality that afflicts the human race, or is it just an expression of the historical totality of actual human sins? The question has been much debated in contemporary Catholic theology. Even putting aside Augustine's literal interpretation of Genesis and his "fall" theory, theologians have struggled with the concept of original sin as a reality present to humans upon their entrance into this world, something in addition to personal human sins. Since the middle ages Anselm and Aquinas portrayed this state as an absence of sanctifying grace. Modern theologians since Vatican II have been divided in affirming or denying this reality. In his examination of this question, Brian O. McDermott, S.J., reviews the positions of a number of theologians on each side. To gain some insight into the concerns of contemporary Catholic theologians we will review some proposals for and against the existence of original sin as "distinct reality."[42]

On the one side are "situationalists," such as Karl Rahner, his pupil Karl Heinz-Weger, and Peter Schoonenberg, who struggle to find an interpretation of Trent's insistence that a real guilt is transmitted to humanity prior to individual sin. On the other side are the "personalists," like Urs Baumann and Alfred Vanneste, who claim that no such reality exists, and that what we are dealing with from the start is personal sin. The terms "situationalists" and "personalists" are the designations of a Dutch theologian, George Vandervelde, who conducted a review of contemporary studies on original sin. The labels are convenient, but do not really delineate two distinct philosophical positions. Rather they designate the main concerns, or theological axes, around which the arguments of the two groups seemed to revolve.[43]

Using existentialist language, the situationalists speak of humans being "thrown" into a situation in which their freedom is conditioned by two opposing factors. First, because of God's universal saving will, there is present to all humans the moment they enter the world an offer of divine love, sanctifying grace. This is Rahner's famous concept of the "supernatural existential." However, Rahner also supports an absence of holiness in humanity that should not be, prior to individual moral decision. This is due to something that happened historically to and by humanity. As a result there is an "analogous" guilt present in the human condition. In each person's life, one or the other side of this situation is ratified, by personal sin, or by faith and love. This "original sin" is a mystery that the human mind cannot grasp.[44]

Rahner's position always maintained, theoretically at least, that without baptism or its equivalent, the result of original sin was damnation. However, he first mitigated this with baptism of desire, to take care of worthy individuals outside of Christianity, and finally he proposed a "natural sacrament" working due to the saving grace of Christ, to rescue infants who die without baptism.[45]

Weger's approach is very similar to that of Rahner. He struggles to explain how original sin results in real guilt. Original sin is the absence of that transcendental grace, sanctifying grace, offered to humanity, but somehow blocked by the sinfulness of others. So, just as for Aquinas, it is a privation of grace. Both Rahner and Schoonenberg also support this position. But now, Weger claims that it is more than an absence, because the lack of holiness in a being especially designed to receive that holiness is not just the absence of a finite good. This condition of unholiness, he claims, can be called real, but analogous, guilt. One is born into the world and into a historical sinful situation, says Weger. Original sin is not a static situation that occurs at birth, it grows in time as we participate in sinful humanity. It is an *existential,* an intrinsic dimension of our free existence.

Schoonenberg has a similar existentialist view. Original sin was not some catastrophic sin of the first man; rather it refers to the innumerable sins of all humanity, taken collectively throughout history. Transmission occurs because humans are situated in sin. Again, the situation is an *existential,* which means that it is constitutive of being human. The human race has a solidarity in sin.[46]

On the other side of this debate are the "personalists," most of whom reduce original sin to the factual universality of actual sin in the world.[47] Urs Baumann is on an entirely different wavelength from those seeking some way to favorably interpret the statements of Trent. He totally denies that there is anything like an objective, empirical ground for our sinful condition. He centers his thought on the human person, on his or her responsibility, guilt, and radical need for redemption. The core of the person cannot be objectified, he claims; sin is basically incomprehensible. The doctrine of original sin is telling us about human nature, and the radicality, totality, and universality of personal sin. It is radically rooted in the freedom of the person. It affects the total person, robbing them of real freedom. Finally, the doctrine is revealing the universality of sin; there is a human solidarity in sin. One cannot find a ground for sin except in the personal core of freedom in each individual.

Alfred Vanneste, another "personalist," plays on some of the same themes. He is deeply convinced of the strict universality of personal sin. As soon as a child becomes a moral person, he states, that child will freely, but inevitably, sin in the first act of the will. He calls this a "law" but at the same time insists that moral decisions are free. Vanneste admits that there is a paradox here, but he claims that it is at the heart of authentic Catholic teaching. The statement "All humans are born in original sin" means that all are sinners from the first moment they are human. All adults are sinners and all pre-adults are "virtual sinners," he says. But sin is due to misused freedom, and the person still has the capacity to love God above all things even after sinning, "because it is this capability which constitutes the religious essence of the human being."[48] Vanneste claims that no one is saved unless he or she cooperates with divine grace. This then excludes children, whose fate is unknown.[49]

Other theologians included in the "personalist" category include Juan Luis Segundo, who reflects on evil and evolution, trying to relate sin to the physical principle of entropy. This principle states that a closed physical system will run down, as time goes on, leaving matter in its lowest energy state. Segundo sees an analogy of continuity between evolution which works in opposition to entropy on the lower material level, and evolution and sin which are in opposition in the human domain. He stresses the universal saving will of God in Christ, and sees in the doctrine of original sin a recognition of a powerful human solidarity, but not one that implies human guilt before personal sin.[50]

A review of the situationalist and personalist positions conducted by G. Vandervelde clarifies the significant aspects of each approach.[51] The situationalists make clear the involuntary aspect of original sin, present to all before free decisions, and stress the universality of God's grace, he notes, but they also identify original sin with a privation of sanctifying grace. Vandervelde is concerned that in doing so they have given up the religious concept of original sin as the radical unwillingness to open oneself to God, Augustine's *aversio a Deo*. Further, he considers that the situationalists have abstracted the concept of "situation" from the concept of person to the extent that it does not seem to involve the person's freedom or any specific historical action. And finally, he says, their approach relativizes the need for baptism, reducing the sacrament's effect to entrance into the Church as the medium of the fullness of grace necessary for salvation.[52]

Vandervelde is even less happy with the "personalists," who stress individual responsibility and freedom in the relationship of person to Creator, but tend toward a kind of fatalism in their insistence that all will sin. To know that all individuals will in fact sin would require a supra-historical standpoint, he notes, which it is impossible to claim. Vanneste's whole theory rides on such an assertion, says Vandervelde, and the depth dimension of original sin is entirely missing.[53]

Baumann tries to find the authentic meaning of original sin in radical human freedom. But this, says Vandervelde, appears to contradict his contention that Scripture sees sin as an already-being-there. Vandervelde finds the theories of the two groups to be so far apart that he sees no possibility for synthesis.[54]

After reviewing the work of Vandervelde and others, Brian McDermott concludes that the great efforts of Catholic theologians to show how original sin is true but analogous guilt require that any revised theory of original sin retain both the situational privation of grace and the negative involuntary, the *aversio a Deo.* In his judgment, the "self-enslavement which is personal sin is grounded in both self (freedom) and a negative involuntary."[55]

A Modern Synthesis

A few years ago, Stephen J. Duffy attempted a synthesis of contemporary investigations of original sin.[56] His thought revolves around the personalist and situationalist axes discussed above, and incorporates insights from modern psychology, sociology, and Christology. His careful review of the history of the doctrine reveals the origins of the traditional version in Augustine's anti-Gnostic myth. God is absolved from responsibility for the obvious evil in the world and humanity is saddled with a burden of guilt. Duffy desires to save the treasure contained in the Adamic myth and the Augustinian symbolism, steering a course between a naive fundamentalism and moral rationalism. To do this he centers the meaning of the doctrine not in some interpretation of a terrible hereditary guilt but in the sinful situation humanity finds itself in and confesses in its worship. Ricoeur is quoted with approval as he reminds us that when we speculate about original sin we should not expect to reach full intelligibility, since it is, after all, only a rationalized myth about the mystery of evil.[57]

Duffy rehearses the human situation, noting our self-transcending spirit that enables us to be creative and achieve, or to be destructive. The human spirit is caught between the reach for the transcendent and the finitude and pain of our existence. Out of these two things, says Duffy, transcendence and finitude, is born anxiety. This *angst* then is a pre-condition for sin and causes us to seek our own interests at the cost of everything else.

> Because the wolf is always at the door, we are especially anxious about our future, about money, food, enemies, land,

power, status, about not having enough or losing what we have. In this anxiety we are driven to seek apotheosis and security at the expense of others.[58]

This anxiety is not itself sin, but the temptation to sin. With conversion, it becomes the source of self-achievement.

In addition to this ontological state of insecurity, which is constitutive of finitude and freedom, there is our distance from God as evidenced by our inability to grasp the divine except in faith and hope. Our reach for the divine can result in allegiance to false gods, and misplaced loyalties. This then is the human predicament: drawn toward the good and unable to achieve it as we would, the unruly appetites (traditionally called concupiscence) keep pulling us toward the satisfaction of selfish interests.

To further elucidate the concept of concupiscence, Duffy draws on Freudian psychology. Freud called attention to the unconscious in which the *id*, a pool of unconscious libidinal energies controlled by the "pleasure principle," clamors for instant gratification. The emerging conscious ego tries to police the *id* and to put off instant gratification for future or morally desirable goals. One of the clarifications emerging from this analysis is the realization that concupiscence is not the result of sin. It can be an enticement to sin, but it can also foster creative drives. This psychological explanation for our biological heritage reveals that this struggle is a natural human condition. We are born fallen, says Duffy.[59]

The third aspect of Freudian theory is the incorporation into our psyches of parents' and teachers' values, reinforced by rewards and punishments. These become part of our unconscious orientation, as the *superego*, long before we are competent to understand them.

Duffy likes a suggestion made by Sebastian Moore that we should understand the fall as the birth of consciousness and the dawning awareness of God.[60] At some moment as children we become aware that we are in a world in which there is pain,

anxiety, and guilt. We are nostalgic for the psychic womb where
there was peace and security, and find ourselves unable to return
to it. Instead we can only move ahead. As Christian consciousness dawns, we realize that it is the kingdom for which we yearn,
and it can only be reached through the grim passage of death.

The transmission of original sin, Duffy proposes, can best
be approached through the insights of the social sciences. In
addition to being a result of our finite human natures, original
sin is also passed on through culture. It "refers to the whole
process of socialization by which a human being enters the
world, including birth and interpersonal relationships."[61]
Original sin is a dynamic historical dimension of being in a
sinful world and growing within it. It is not at first instance a
conscious decision. It is not imitation of Adam's sin, which
Trent wanted to deny: it is pre-conscious and universal. Thus,
there is no theological need to worry about direct biological
decent from Adam, monogenism, to support its universality,
which Trent also wished to assert.

The whole problem of original sin has been enlightened by
the realization of what Duffy calls "the eschatological dimension." In his words,

> This eschatological thrust incorporates a more processive, evo-
> lutionary perspective from which original sin is viewed not as
> the disastrous residue of some primal crime but as a present
> conflict between our history and the dynamics of the ultimate.
> It is the contradiction between what humans are and what
> they are called to become in Christ.[62]

This is the Christological factor we spoke of earlier. Duffy
reminds us of Rahner's theology of grace, which makes clear
that we live in a graced world. Christ is the center; sin is a background, only really understood when we realize the distance
between what we are and what we are called to be. To call this
situation "original sin," says Duffy, is to stretch analogy to the
breaking point. Original sin is a "code word" for a situation that

is natural for humans as disordered and incomplete beings. He notes that this view is in keeping with the theodicy of Irenaeus, proposed in the second century. Irenaeus said that God made the world as a testing ground, a place for human growth. Made to the image of God, with intelligence, humans are meant to become the likeness of God. This Irenaean myth, Duffy feels, is an improved alternate to the myth of Augustine.[63]

Duffy's proposals and the Irenaean myth are in keeping with the conclusion of contemporary Catholic theology that the universality of grace is more than a match for the universality of sin. "Where sin increased, grace abounded all the more" (Rom 5:20). Adam as type and Christ as antitype are not an equal match. As a result, there is no absolute need for baptism, because being redeemed in Christ overcomes being born in original sin.

> Baptism cannot "remove" original sin understood as a mode of existence where we are driven by anxiety, at the mercy of the unconscious, and bound in historical solidarity with evil, all of which leave us primed for evil.[64]

Baptism is best understood as initiation into the Christian community where there can be growth in a graced relationship with God. Duffy might also have noted that one of the best reasons for infant baptism is that it reminds the community of the complete gratuitousness of God's love, in that it is given to humans before we are capable of doing anything by ourselves. This, for Paul is the meaning of God's act in Christ: he redeems the ungodly.[65]

The reinterpretation proposed by Stephen Duffy is representative of a contemporary Catholic view that does justice to the intents and concerns of the traditional doctrine and is based on modern Scripture studies, current theology, and an evolutionary worldview. In addition, it should be clear from the other examples given of post-Vatican II theological studies on original sin and evolution that theologians have absorbed the lessons of the Council and modern scriptural exegesis, and have moved away from the restrictions of a literal interpretation of the first chapters of Genesis and the Augustinian story of original sin. Some directly accept the theory of human evolution, while others, without saying whether they did so, proposed theories that were consistent with an evolutionary view. Gone is the concept of humanity created in paradise free from suffering and death. Gone is a world changed in its very nature due to a terrible sin of an historical Adam which damned all his descendants. Affirmed and proclaimed is the scriptural revelation that humanity comes into the world in need of God's grace and salvation, without which it can do nothing to reach God. Theological opinion now stresses that it is through the grace of Jesus Christ that we are reconciled to God. There is available then sufficient consensus among Catholic theologians on the meaning of original sin for us today.

Duffy's proposal is incomplete, however, in that it provides no insight into the evolutionary heritage that produces the human condition of anxiety that he describes so well in psychological terms. We will return to this need in our final chapter.

Finally, the Catholic view on original sin is still not totally home free. There is still Augustine's concern for the source of the terrible natural evils present in the world. Who is responsible: God, a Manichean equal evil power, or humanity, as Augustine himself concluded? Removing Adam's sin as the cause of physical evil seems to leave God, at least indirectly, responsible for it. Some amelioration of the mystery of evil awaits another theological advance, perhaps a reconsideration of the divine nature itself, as suggested by the phenomenon of evolution itself. Before approaching this question we need to understand just what story evolution is telling us. We need to address that question first from a scientific point of view, and then from a new theological perspective.

4
Evolution: Problem or Clue?

In recent years, a number of public opinion polls have revealed that about half of adult Americans believe that "God created man pretty much in his present form at one time within the last 10,000 years."[1] At the same time the scientific establishment almost unanimously holds that humans evolved from lower life forms over billions of years. This is a problem.

But *should* there be a problem? And if the answer is no, why does the problem exist? The answer to the first question *is* no! The answer to the second is multi-faceted, and conceals numerous confusions, misunderstandings, and, frankly, some downright ignorance. We need to explore some of the reasons people don't accept the theory of evolution, to see if we can clear up some of the confusion. Acceptance of the theory of evolution should not be a problem for Christians, and failure to give the theory its due is negatively impacting our theological understanding. As Aquinas said, mistakes about nature are mistakes about God.[2]

One of the reasons Christians have resisted the theory of evolution is the belief that it is contrary to the Bible. We dealt with that concern in chapter 3, where we saw that today's biblical scholars realize that the inspired witness to the experience of God that we call the Bible does not teach science or the origin of life, but does teach about our relationship to God and

71

how to live. Once one has grasped the nature of Scripture, and let go of the idea that all its stories are literally true, the biggest problem for Christians is removed.

However, the scriptural objection to evolution is often coupled with a confusion about the nature of science. This mistaken impression is not limited to non-scientists; some scientists themselves are caught in the same confusion. Science in its fullest sense has to do with the application of a group of techniques for investigating nature. Scientists propose theories to describe nature's workings, they make predictions, and then compare these with experimental results. By iterating on these procedures they improve their understanding of how the universe works. A key phrase in that last statement is "how the universe works." Not "why" the universe exists, or what it means, but "how it works." Science deals with what philosophers call "secondary causation," how one thing flows from another in time. It does not deal with "primary causation," the ontological question of why anything exists in the first place, and is sustained in existence, the question of the dependency of contingent things. It is religious experience and thought that deal with meaning, value, and the ontological question.

The collection of techniques called scientific thinking does not allow for supernatural intervention in going from one step to another. The methods are reductionist, materialistic, rational, and they have been remarkably successful. Scientists find that nature operates according to laws, and formulates those laws, if possible, in mathematical form. They have no means of determining why the laws are there to be found, or of learning anything about the law giver. Therefore, there is nothing that scientists can ever discover that will prove or disprove the existence of God or divine creation.

This confusion concerning the nature of science is sometimes coupled, by scientists who are anti-religious, with another error that has been called "scientism."[3] Scientism is the belief that scientific knowledge is the only kind of knowledge.

Adherents to this belief consider that if something cannot be verified scientifically, it is just subjective opinion, and so without any objective value. Most scientists know better. And most scientists, knowing better, don't make disparaging remarks about religion.

Unfortunately, the scientists we hear most about are those few popularizers who don't recognize that the question of ontological causation remains after science has examined how things work. They also subscribe to "scientism," believing scientific knowledge to be the only knowledge that counts.[4] Some of these writers make claims that findings in physics, or cosmology, or biology disprove the existence or need for a Creator God.[5] If they convince religious people that science is demonstrating their religious beliefs to be false, it is not surprising that people conclude that science is anti-religion. If one understands the theory of evolution to include the denial of the existence of God, it *should* be rejected. However, most scientists and many religious people understand that the theory of biological evolution deals with species change through mutation and natural selection, and says nothing about God. We hope it is becoming clear that if one really understands what science is all about, and how it works, there should be no conflict between science and religion.

The other side of the coin is the confusion caused by religious fundamentalists who consider that their religious knowledge includes scientific conclusions drawn from the Bible. Creationists attempt to gain scientific knowledge from the creation story as understood from a literal reading of the Bible. A recent version of creationism called "Creation Science" has developed out of a Seventh Day Adventist background, and has been surprisingly successful in convincing many people that direct creation, within the last ten to twenty-five thousand years, is a scientific theory.[6] Creation Science is poor science devoted to supporting the biblical story of creation. Its support in the wider scientific community is almost nil. The story of its rise, by Professor of the History of Science, Ronald Numbers, at the University of Wisconsin, is fascinating. The Seventh Day Adventists preach a final meeting with Christ on the "seventh day." It's hard to believe in a seventh day, they worry, if the first six biblical days did not really happen! Creation Scientists are easy targets for the science popularizers, many of whom write as though all religious people were fundamentalists. This mistaken assumption fans the flames of antagonism between religion and science.[7]

But why are the flames of controversy on the matter of evolution so easy to kindle and keep alight? Besides scientists and religious people who overstep the bounds of their disciplines, there are other reasons. One that looms large is the scientific difficulty of the subject. One can demonstrate the theory of gravity quickly, accurately, and repeatedly in simple laboratory experiments. The data supporting the evolution of life over three to four billion years is largely unavailable. No one was around to see the changes over billions of years. There are fossil remains, but these are relatively rare. To become a fossil, to be preserved by gradually turning to stone, requires special conditions of burial and preservation. The fossil must then come to the surface again and be discovered. Between the time that life forms died, fossils were formed, and then discovered, the continents on which they had lived were reshaped and repositioned on the globe as the earth's crust rose and fell along vast cracks and boundaries. This is the same movement or plate tectonics that has caused the rise of mountain ranges and that continues today to produce active volcanoes. Today many fossils are located far from where the organisms originally lived. Later in this chapter we will talk about the amazing amount of information that we do have that supports evolutionary theory, but we recognize here at the outset that demonstration of support for the theory is massively more difficult than laboratory physics experiments. Added to the difficulty is the fact that, according to a recent poll, American adults have a low level of scientific literacy.[8] The data suggest that interest in science is low, and that science is not being well taught in grade school and high school, a challenge for American educators.

In spite of the subject's difficulty, it is time that Christians did their homework and looked at the implications of the theory of evolution without fear. If the universe and human beings did evolve, then this is the way God works as Creator. Just as the work of art reveals something of the artist, so the wonders of the universe reveal something of the Creator. Because of this, religion and science should be in contact with each other, in conversation, so that some consonance between the two disciplines can be explored. Christians are called to love God not just with their whole hearts, but with their whole minds (Mt 22:37), and this necessitates being open to human knowledge of the universe, one of the signs of our times, and searching that knowledge for the revealing presence of God.

Evolution's Story

Before we can consider the implications of the story of the universe we need to have heard that story ourselves. The story can be told in many different ways. For our purposes, a brief description of how scientists today understand the buildup with time of particles, atoms, stars and planets seems appropriate. These events were followed by the evolution of life, from the simplest to the most advanced forms. The human species developed out of the primate order of mammals.[9]

In telling this story the term evolution will refer to the whole process, from particles to humans. It is when the whole is considered that the beauty and the vast explanatory power of the concept becomes most apparent. Scientifically, there are evolutionary theories for the various chapters: a theory of the evolution of elements, a theory of biological evolution, and theories of human evolution, for example. Scientists in their individual disciplines usually leave the grand overviews to philosophers of science and popular science writers.

The story begins with a bang, the "Big Bang," some fifteen billion years ago. This is perhaps not the best analogy, because it means to describe that the cosmos began at a singularity, a fuzzy point without space or time. Space and time began with the entire mass of the universe compressed into an unimaginably small volume with fantastically high density and temperature. These early temperatures and densities were such that atoms as we know them could not exist. The universe did not explode with matter thrown out into space; rather space itself came into existence and expanded, and time, for this cosmic epoch, began.[10]

As the unbelievably hot and dense mass of the universe expanded and cooled, initially more rapidly, then less so, the fundamental particles of nature formed out of the hot "soup," and in successive stages of cooling, neutrons and protons the fundamental constituents of atoms were formed. Then came the simplest atoms themselves, hydrogen and helium.

One of the successes of big bang theory is the successful prediction of the relative abundance of the end products of the initial three minutes, a universe of roughly three-quarters hydrogen and one-quarter helium.[11] Another is a background radiation in the sky as a result of the Big Bang. Its presence and wavelength had been predicted, and were discovered in 1965.

Great swirls of hydrogen and helium were drawn together by gravity. As massive amounts were compressed, the temperature increased until fusion reactions began. From hydrogen came more helium and then, in a series of different and intricate chains of formation, the heavier elements were created. The main job of the stars is element creation, and those very elements, made billions of years ago, are present in us and everything we see. Stars of different sizes, temperatures, and compositions were formed. Some burned for a few million years, some like our sun will burn for about ten billion years, still others will last one hundred billion years. When some very large stars have used up their fuel they collapse, oscillate, and explode in what is called a supernova. When this happens the heavier elements are formed in the waves of matter blown into space. There they condense into masses of gas from which new stars are born. There have been several generations of stars before most of those that now exist. The nuclear processes that take place in the evolution of elements have been worked out by scientists, and the results agree with the abundance of elements determined by measurements on earth, in meteorites, and from analysis of the spectra of stars, interstellar gas and dust.[12]

In our galaxy, vast irregular masses of gas and dust are collapsing and forming suns and associated planets, an estimated one new solar system per month. In the entire observable universe, which contains at least a hundred billion galaxies, there are perhaps a hundred solar systems being formed every second.[13] Think a moment about the magnitude of time and space involved in just that portion of God's creation we know something about.

Our earth was formed by accretion of matter circling the sun about 4.5 billion years ago. Two hundred million years later it was probably still undergoing meteor bombardment. It may have been studded with volcanic islands and covered with carbon dioxide. Most of the original rock formations have been destroyed by geologic activity. About eighty percent of the atmosphere seeped out from the interior of the planet in the first million years of its life. The rest was slowly released over the next 4.4 billion years.

Continental drifts have been calculated back 700 million years. The supercontinent Pangaea came together about 200 million years ago and then broke apart, after which the continents we know were gradually formed and positioned. Recent studies suggest that atmospheric oxygen accumulated about two billion years ago. The present twenty percent oxygen level is the result of photosynthesis, and was reached about 1.5 billion years ago.[14] And photosyntheses means life! What about life?

The Facts of Life

Life has existed on earth for at least 3.5 billion years. Fossil bacteria have been found in Australian rocks of that age. The exact method of its formation is unknown. It may have started with short chains of nucleotides with stronger chemical bonds than most, developing feedback loops and encouraging each other, or it may have arrived on earth from space, which pushes the "how life began" problem to somewhere else. In any case, all living things use the same four chemical bases to make the same twenty amino acids. And the bases combine together in groups of three, a triplet code for the formation of amino acids. The code is the same in all organisms. The chains of molecules for assembling amino acids into proteins are also essentially the same. All contemporary organisms carry their genetic information in nucleic acids called RNA and DNA, and use essentially the same genetic code. The code specifies the amino acid sequences of all the proteins that make up organisms. The only thing that differentiates one organism from another is the message itself spelled out in the DNA. It is the message that makes a bacterium or a human being.[15] The message for human being is spelled out in long strands of DNA shaped like a double helix and called chromosomes. Packages of DNA spaced along the chromosomes contain inheritable traits, and are called genes.

There are many small differences in the DNA within a population. A mutation is a change in the order of base pairings in a little strip of DNA. These are caused by radiation, chemical agents, crossovers of chromosomes touching at a common point, and the splitting and pairing of chromosomes in sexual generation. Some of the end products in a species are better adapted to the environment and these are "selected" for survival. The process involves a great deal of chance. Until recently, many biologists thought that there was nothing in nature to produce progress, since only chance was involved, and so concluded that the evolution of human intelligence was a fluke, an accident. However, in recent years, scientists have discovered that there is a natural propensity for self-organization at many levels in nature, which can provide the rationale for evolution of more complex systems.[16]

The path of evolution is marked by development of more complex systems, but at first it seemed to take forever. For billions of years after life began it remained unicellular. About 530 million years ago, according to the fossil evidence, there was an explosion of forms of life. About 350 million years ago the first amphibians came out of the sea to live on land. Shortly thereafter the first reptile appeared. The dinosaur arrived about 225 million years ago, the first mammal about 200 million years ago, and then, 145 million years ago, the first bird.

A striking feature in the history of life and its forms is the presence of at least five major extinctions where many or almost all of the species existing at the time disappeared. These have all occurred in the last half-billion years. They are thought to have been due to changes in climate and in sea level. The earth's atmosphere may have been altered by gases released through movements of the earth's crust, volcanic eruptions, lava flows, perhaps combined with asteroid strikes (especially for the extinction of the dinosaurs, sixty-five million years ago). After each extinction, a burst of new species appeared, which rushed in to fill all the niches that could support life.[17] Two hundred and forty-five million years ago a great extinction eliminated ninety-six percent of the marine animals. In came the dinosaurs.

Let us look a bit at the dinosauria as an example of the evidence that suggests if life on earth had an aim it was not creation of human beings. Dinosaurs first appear in the fossil record 225 million years ago. They disappeared relatively abruptly, connected somehow with the strike on earth of a six-mile-diameter asteroid, sixty-five million years ago. Their reign began assisted by some natural catastrophe and ended in the same way. They were the dominant beings on earth for 160 million years. (For comparison purposes, our species has been in existence for a little over 100,000 years.) Three hundred different species of dinosaurs have been identified so far, and it is estimated that at least three times that number remain to be found. Description of a new species appears in the scientific literature about every seven weeks. Different species evolved during their reign, from huge pea-brained vegetarians to human-sized, razor-clawed meat-eaters, with the estimated intelligence of an ostrich.[18] An asteroid strike of the magnitude involved in their extinction is likely on average every 100 million years. But there is some probability that the next one may arrive in 10,000 years, or next year.[19]

With the end of the dinosaurs came the rise of the mammals. The order of mammals that we belong to evolved about this time, the primates. Primates are thought to have emerged from small (mouse-sized), nocturnal, insect-eating, shrew-like animals that probably lived in trees.[20] About five to eight million years ago, according to the fossil record, hominids (humans and their direct ancestors) and apes split off from a common ancestor. The hominid line is believed to be closest to that of the chimpanzees, making them a cousin race. The earliest hominids were the *Australopithecines* who lived for several million years.[21] The ancestral trail for the last four million years is hotly contested, but a recent "mainstream" assessment proposes three genera, or closely related species of hominids, containing about a dozen species in that period, leading to *Homo sapiens:* two species of *Australopithecines,* four *Paranthropus,* and seven in the genus *Homo.*[22] These last species are *Homo habilis, rudolfensis, ergaster, erectus, heidelbergensis, neanderthalensis,* and *sapiens.* The story of the last two million years includes increasing brain size, tool development, bi-pedalism, language development, and finally evidence in cave art and artifacts suggesting minds very like our own some forty thousand years ago. The facts of life are a far cry from the story of Adam and Eve.

Molecular biology is now providing another means to investigate the evolutionary history of organisms. Differences among species arise from mutations in the DNA, and the DNA can be studied to note the similarities and differences, and to assess the periods of time required for such changes to occur. These studies confirm that the species closest to human beings is the chimp. Over 99.5 percent of our DNA is the same. Chimps and humans are about as closely related as horses and donkeys. The evolutionary split of apes and humans some eight million years ago is also confirmed. Scientists are encouraged by how well the data from molecular biology agree with the fossil record.[23]

We should mention at this point that scientists are finding that human beings are much closer to other primates than we would like to believe.

> It was long assumed that there is a huge behavioral chasm between humans and animals. Thirty years of work on primates have changed that view. We now know that higher primates—and some other mammals—have complex behaviors that are learned, differ among populations, and can be transmitted from one generation to the next. Even if these patterns of behaviors are not in themselves cultural, all their attributes are needed for the evolution of culture.[24]

Chimps are to some degree self-aware. They submit to higher rank. "Females defer to males. They cherish their parents. They care for their young. They have a kind of patriotism, and defend the group against outsiders. They share food. They abhor incest."[25] There is even something like a code of ethics among them.

Evolution continues, although human evolution is now at somewhat of a stalemate. Evolution requires population fragmentation, and at present the human population is rapidly becoming denser and intermixed. So the conditions for significant evolutionary change don't exist.[26] It has been speculated that colonization of space would provide the requisite condition for human evolution, and might be necessary to insure that a future extinction does not include our species.[27]

The earth will be subject to future extinctions. Life proliferates, but life is fragile. The diversity of life is very great, which is an unappreciated resource. There are probably over 100 million species of life, with new species being found every day. Among known species, the animals number 1,032,000. This number includes 751,000 species of insects (290,000 kinds of beetles), and 4,000 mammals. There are 248,000 species of plants, and probably millions of kinds of bacteria.[28] The species are intertwined in each ecosystem, and dependent upon each other. Plants owe their lives to insects, who turn the soil around their roots, and decompose dead tissue into nutrients required for continual growth.[29] Unfortunately, we are in the midst of a sixth great extinction, one caused by humanity, by destruction of habitats, displacement by introduced species, and chemical pollutants. Species destroyed each year number 27,000, seventy-four each day, three per hour. It is estimated that a twenty percent extinction of total global biodiversity is possible by the year 2022, at the current rate of environmental destruction.[30]

Finally, in this encapsulated summary of the facts of life, it is important to note that every year scientific information is moving us closer to the realization that the universe is filled with life. We know that the laws of nature—gravity, atomic spectra, etc.— are the same throughout the known universe. Astronomers have identified more than four dozen simple organic compounds in interstellar space. Planets have now been found around a number of other stars.[31] NASA scientists have announced that life has been found in meteors that came from the planet Mars, and the evidence is undergoing intense scrutiny. But, whether this announcement holds up or not, the likelihood of life existing elsewhere in the universe is increasingly judged to be great. The handwriting is on the wall. Listen to a Nobel Prize winner in biology, writing in 1994.

> Organic carbon compounds are everywhere. They make up 20 percent of interstellar dust, and interstellar dust makes up 0.1 percent of galactic matter. In this organic cloud, which pervades the universe, life is almost bound to arise, in a molecular form not very different from its form on Earth, wherever physical conditions are similar to those that prevailed on our planet some four billion years ago. This conclusion seems to me inescapable.[32]

Evolution's Clues

Creation reveals the Creator. It is fair then to speculate on the implications of the universe's story for our understanding of the nature of God and creation. It is a very different tale from that in the book of Genesis. The world as we know it did not come into existence in an instant. The first humans were not created at a word, in a privileged state, and located in a paradise devoid of suffering and death. Our ancestors arose to consciousness in bands of hunter-gatherers much like those primitive groups of this type that have been disappearing in the last few centuries. Death was not the result of sin. Death has been around for perhaps a billion years on our planet. It arrived when unicellular life evolved propagation by sex. Sexual unions vastly increased the mix of genes, but now instead of cells multiplying and splitting apart, new generations carried modified life forms forward, and death claimed their ancestors.

The biggest difference between the story in Genesis 1–3, and the story of the universe told in the previous section, is the importance in the latter of time. God's creative action took time—vast amounts of time. Matter and time are intrinsically related, and they evolved in understandable steps. Apparently, vast periods of time were necessary. The painfully slow evolution of life, spreading in great diversity into all available niches, trying out all possible avenues of advance, the huge role of chance, the stumbling advances to greater complexity, all these things suggest a divine nature at odds with the omnipotent God of classical theism. The universe, as we know it, was not created in an instant of absolute coercive power. The creeping advance of matter and life, the spread of probabilities, the diversity of approaches, all suggest some sharing of power between Creator and creatures. It is as though divinity labored to persuade, to lure creatures forward, creatures who sometimes responded to the invitation, and sometimes did not. But God obviously did not tire of the game, even after being resisted for billions of years. The spectacle of evolution suggests God at work with stubborn individuals who had some power of self-determination, urging them to creatively advance. The universe's story is suggesting that divine power is different from what we have imagined. It is like the power of love, persuasive, patient, and persistent. Why would God create in the evolutionary way if a better way were possible?

These characteristics of evolution, when considered in relation to the divine nature, move counter to the classical theism of the middle ages, counter to the Greek philosophical categories adopted by early Christianity: those of omnipotence, immutability, the eternal and the absolute. They suggest shared power, and free determination by creatures allowed, or required, to share in their own destiny. The idea of creation by persuasion, surprisingly, suggests a Creator much closer to the biblical God of love than that of classical theism.

When we focus our view on creation itself, it is apparent that it is not the result of an exact plan. Over ninety-nine percent of all species that ever lived are now extinct. The rise of intelligence could have occurred in a species other than our own. Neither is creation all good in the moral sense. The universe contains finite creatures in competition, where one's gain is another's loss. It contains chance blunders of matter and energy that produce natural disasters, and violence of immense magnitude. Countless individuals and species have suffered and perished. When sentience and feeling arose, and pain became real, it produced evil. When the universe became conscious of itself, in human beings, it produced sin. And humans may not be the only sinners in God's universe.

There are things evident in the evolved universe that one strains to find consistent with belief in a loving God. Consider over a hundred million years of dinosaurs, half of which savagely hunted and ate the others. To what end? Was God pleased in some way with this spectacle? What about insects that have evolved to be parasites living within and destroying other life? Anyone who has watched the wonderful nature shows put on television by *National Geographic* has been startled, or perhaps horrified, by the seemingly endless array of barbarous predatory life living on our planet. Such things bewilder the believer trying to relate them to the Christian God of love. Is the God of nature a being of awful and savage indifference, totally inscrutable in divine purpose and enjoyment? Does the existence of nature negate belief in the God we call our Father? Some people think so. Are these things we have been discussing reasonably the products of a God who can do anything? Perhaps our ideas about the divine nature and activity are too simplistic and historically conditioned. Are there acceptable alternative views for a Christian?

We noted above that the elements of chance in the evolution of the human species belies an exact divine plan, existing from all eternity to produce the human race. There are no doubt divine plans, but we must face the possibility that our role in them has not been central. Evolution's story suggests that the divine plan is to move the universe toward greater complexity and greater consciousness, because that is what has happened. In this Christians can see creation of the conditions that allow for production of greater worth, the values of mutual love, responsibility and union that are the revealed qualities of divinity. Perhaps divinity is luring the evolving universe toward its own likeness.

The magnitude of the universe in space and time indicates that nature is God's great work. Whatever God's plans, they are being worked out in continual creation, over billions of years and unimaginable distances. Now on earth, with the emergence of human beings, evolution has become aware of itself. We can try to ascertain the divine purposes and to aid them. We have the opportunity to become God's hands. In our own small way we can be "co-creators" of values revealed and discovered.[33]

Our earth and all its species are mutually related. We see now how the good of one segment influences the well-being, the wholesomeness of the other, and of the whole. For example, if the insects don't turn the soil and decompose dead tissue into nutrients the plants won't grow. If plants don't grow animal life cannot exist. The continual existence of our species requires concern for the well-being of the whole. The move to preserve our ecology is both timely and necessary for survival. Evolution has demonstrated how God works in the world. Divinity has worked slowly and well. But our earth at present is dominated by human technology, and the well-being of all its species is under human control. Humanity with its industrial pollution capability and its nuclear weapons arsenal has the capability to destroy in a relatively few years what God has taken billions of years to call into being. If the divine efforts have taken so much time, and humans seem able to thwart them so rapidly, the call in Genesis for humans to till this garden earth takes on new urgency. It suggests that we are called to participate, to assist, as caretakers of our world. All of a sudden we have realized that we are responsible for the world and its well-being. To be good stewards and faithful caretakers of the gifts that we have been entrusted with is consistent with the message of Scripture.

Another clue to the divine nature and purpose is present in current assessments of the possibility of life elsewhere in the universe. A number of things suggest it is likely that the universe is filled with intelligent life. First, its size is vast and it has been evolving for billions of years. Second, astronomical data confirm that the far distant galaxies contain the same elements and molecules that make up our own solar system. The distant stars are glowing by means of the same nuclear processes that fuel our sun. In addition, the observed movements of distant stellar objects demonstrate that they obey the same laws of gravitation that move our planets. Is it reasonable to suppose that God would call into being billions of stars and galaxies and yet limit life to one obscure planet? It seems more likely that many species have been called toward the divine life, perhaps long before our own became conscious. Teilhard de Chardin thought so, and tried to alert his contemporaries to the need for theology to be open to the implications of evolution.

> Considering what we now know about the number of "worlds" and their internal evolution, the idea of a *single* hominized *planet* in the universe has already become in fact (without our generally realizing it) almost as *inconceivable* as that of a man who appeared with no genetic relationship to the rest of the earth's animal population. At an average of (at least) one human race per galaxy, that makes a total of millions of human races dotted all over the heavens. Confronted with this fantastic multiplicity of astral centres of "immortal life," how is theology going to react, if it is to satisfy the anxious expectations and hopes of all who wish to continue to worship God "in spirit and in truth"? It obviously cannot go on much longer offering as the only *dogmatically certain* thesis one

(that of the uniqueness in the universe of terrestrial mankind) which our experience rejects as *improbable*.[34]

We need, said Teilhard, a theology of evolution.

When we consider evolution's time scale, the Church is not old. As Professor Walter Ong, S.J., reminds us, we need to think of the Church in God's real universe, as we know that universe to be.

> In such real-time perspectives, a church founded only some 2000 years ago can be only in its infancy. The church's life would appear to lie mostly in the uncounted years ahead. Thinking of the church as "old" hardly synchronizes it with God's ongoing creation.[35]

Ong's remarks remind one of a recent *New York Times* news poll which reported that one in four American Christians expects the Second Coming of Christ to occur in their life-time.[36] We can bet also that the year 2000 will be marked by predictions of the world's end, and a bit of local hysteria here and there. We really should be wondering how the Church will be doing one hundred thousand or a million years from now. The idea of God bringing the universe to an end in the near future through Christ's second coming is not compatible with the evidence of the divine efforts in the universe for fifteen bil-lion years. The idea that the universe should end because human beings have reached consciousness, and realized their own sinfulness and manifest inability to control their civiliza-tions, could only arise in a species who considered themselves the center and pinnacle of creation. The universe's story sug-gests that this is not the case. The human mind-set is being urged to adjust to the possibility that perhaps we have been called into existence to assist in a greater divine evolutionary plan to move the whole universe toward divinity, to be co-workers, co-creators in bringing about the Kingdom of God among us. Perhaps eschatology needs to be rethought.[37]

Messages to the Church from the universe's story are, first, one of humility, and, second, one of non-exclusivity. The diversity of creatures, creatively moving in myriad directions, each seeking and finding its own individual value, in unimaginable numbers even on our own planet, and likely in even greater quantities elsewhere, is humbling to a species historically insistent upon its own centrality and importance. Church leaders should realize that Scripture and Tradition tell us much less about human nature and destiny than some of their official statements would have the world believe.

Human nature is in many respects in continuity with the primates from which we evolved. And we are still evolving. There is a sense then in which human nature is open-ended. We only know our nature to the point to which we have evolved. What we don't know is what human nature will become. The track of our evolution indicates the operation of chance, and the building upon our reptilian and mammalian ancestors. Biologists emphasize that if evolution were to be run over again, there is little chance that humans would evolve.[38]

The concept of a fixed human nature designed by God has been much used in the natural law approach to moral theology. The laws of nature reflect the laws of God, this system proposes, and violation of nature's laws, or purposes, is deemed to be sinful as a result. This idea that physical processes determine the only proper human ends (physicialism) provides the support for such things as the Church's position on contraception, because interference with the physical purpose of the sex act is considered to violate divine law. The nature of evolution belies this particular version of a natural law approach.

Second, any "exclusive" theology, which in effect suggests that God is only concerned with one group of people on one planet of one small star, is not credible. It is the product of a theology that considers Scripture in a literalist manner, convinced that it provides a comprehensive scientific worldview, and that has not considered the scientific evidence concerning who we are, where we are, and how we got here. These considerations in no way belittle or need interfere with the Church's mission to preach the gospel of our salvation in Jesus Christ. On the contrary, accepting them would enable the Church to speak to educated people today in a manner that would compel respect.

These clues and speculations related to evolution's story need a philosophical underpinning. They need to be supported by a worldview, a framework for thinking about God and creatures and the interaction between the two. This worldview needs to be consistent and coherent, and to help make sense out of revealed truth and the universe's story. Admittedly such a worldview, such a metaphysics (as the theologians call it), is speculative and always open to revision. We are fortunate that there is such a worldview available. Perhaps by reflecting on our religious traditions in its light, a theology of evolution is possible.

5
Toward a Theology of Evolution

Our God should be worthy of worship. That was the trouble with the classical Greek metaphysics adopted and polished by ancient and medieval theologians such as Thomas Aquinas. The Greek idea was that for God to be perfect, God had to be eternal and immutable, outside of time and unchanging. Because, you see, if God were to change, then it had to be for the better or for the worse. If for the better, then God wasn't perfect before, and if for the worse, God was no longer perfect. Now the problem with such a God was that an unchanging God can't be a God who loves and responds to creatures; that requires real relationships. Such a God really cannot be the God of the Bible. Many Catholic theologians have quietly dropped the concepts of classical theism from their work and have let this model quietly slip into disuse.

There have been other philosophical models of divinity around for thousands of years. One model that Christians have found in the writings of such mystics as Julian of Norwich and Meister Eckhart is called "panentheism." The main idea of panentheism is that the whole of the created universe is within God, although God is other than and superior to it. God is both eternal and temporal, and God both includes and transcends the world.[1] But is such a God perfect, and so worthy of worship? It seems that the definition of

"perfect" for divinity needs to be reexamined. In our day that
has been done most notably by philosophers Alfred North
Whitehead and Charles Hartshorne.[2]

Classical theism needs to be modified, says Hartshorne,
because it is too simplistic. Classical theism looked at the categorical opposites such as eternal-temporal, mutable-immutable,
necessary-contingent, infinite-finite, and so on, and decided that
the first of each of these must apply to God for divinity to be perfect, because they don't change. What was overlooked is that
there are some attributes that don't admit of an absolute or ultimate form. It is true that there can be an absolutely greatest
goodness and justice, but there can not be an ultimate beauty or
an absolutely greatest number. Values are subject to incompati-
bilities. For example, a sonnet and a ballad exclude each other's
merits. Beauty is a harmonized variety of objects. Any beautiful
presentation could be superseded by a still greater variety in an
even more beautiful array.

Indeed, God must be the greatest, must be transcendent,
in all categories. But this means modifying description of the
divine so that God is the greatest possible on both sides of the
categorical opposites. The way to do this, said Hartshorne, is
to define perfection as the categorically ultimate form of all
attributes that admit of such form, and the categorically superior form of all attributes that do not admit of an ultimate
form.[3] Therefore, some attributes of divinity will be defined as
absolutes, unchangeable, and others will be defined as superior, without rival, but capable of being exceeded by divinity
itself. The second category of attributes are changeable, and
therefore temporal. In this "Neoclassical Theism" then, God
is defined as that perfect, supremely excellent being, than
which no other individual being could conceivably be greater,
but which itself, could become greater (perhaps by creation
within itself of new constituents).

Theology using this concept of God today generally goes
by the name of "process theology," because in this scheme

God has temporal attributes of love and relationship with creatures, and thus both the universe and God are in a temporal process. Charles Hartshorne developed his "neoclassical" theism in response to the Christian insight that God *is* love. One of its requirements is that the attributes postulated for God must be consistent with that insight.[4]

When theologians begin thinking of God as love they are hampered by the same Greek metaphysics with its concept of divine perfection that we discussed above. Since in the classical view God cannot change, God is not really affected by creatures; therefore, divine love or *agape* is considered to be an abstract divine will for the good of all, the beneficence of God's grace, shining on all like the rays of the sun, and like the sun unaffected by whatever benefited from its light. Actually this is poor physics, and even worse Christian theology.

Where should Christians look for the definition of love? In Scripture, of course: especially in Jesus' teaching, notably in the parables, where he tries to tell us of the Father's love for us. Reflect on the prodigal son, whose father must have kept a constant watch for his return so that Scripture could say: "While he was still a long way off, his father caught sight of him, and was filled with compassion. He ran to his son, embraced him and kissed him" (Lk 15:20). The parables tell us to look to the best of human love to know of the divine love. There is in Scripture no rejection of human love, desire, passion, friendship, or family love. Rather Scripture uses all the forms of love we know to try to express the divine love. It is the couple, husband and wife, that are held out as revelatory of the divine nature. "So God created humankind in his image, in the image of God he created them; male and female he created them" (Gen 1:27).[5]

If then God *is* love, what does this suggest concerning the divine attributes? It suggests that God is personal and relational, temporal, creative and inclusive. And it implies that divinity's relationship with creatures involves their freedom and creativity. Here we are expressing an analogy, that the best we find in the human experience of love is somehow present in the divine nature.

First, love is a relationship between persons, between individuals. It takes more than one. This implies that God is personal, not just "being" itself. It says that God is affected by others; God feels and responds, God suffers and has joy. Our lives are meaningful because they affect the life of God. These attributes are supported by Scripture. Now we are finding them in the metaphysical nature of God and the universe. A God who is love is worthy of worship; a God who is omnipotent, whose power is coercive, is not.

The best way to think of God in this neoclassical model is as a person. Just as we think of ourselves as inhabiting our bodies, we can think of God as the soul of the world, and the world as God's body. We feel the lesser entities of our body, the cells and organs, as they respond to stimuli. God feels each creature more directly than that, because God is causally involved with each creature's creation from instant to instant, giving each the power of creativity and the offer of increased divine presence.[6] Since God feels all creature's feelings, God suffers our pains and enjoys our pleasures. Listening to God as to another person in prayer, the Scriptures, and the liturgy fosters this personal relationship. Another helpful metaphor is God as Mother of the world. Imagine the world as present in the womb of God, created and nourished by divine love.[7]

Second, the divine nature is relational, that is, having a loving relationship with others is a necessity. Thus, loving and creating are divine necessities; God has always created and always will do so. No particular creatures are necessary, but the actuality of some creatures are necessary in the divine life. The presence of beings who can love God of their own free will is a divine goal. In neoclassical theism, it is the nature of divinity to be continually creating. God has always been creating, and always will be creating, without beginning and without end. The ultimate

e self as it comes into existence. This perfect knowledge
e world and perfect love for all creatures then enables
to prepare for each entity a lure for its next moment of
g. The lure consists of a selected spectrum of possible val-
or each individual to consider incorporating into the next
nt of its existence. The divine call is toward love, good-
, truth and beauty. The whole of creation is the loved one,
sponse is evolution.

nan Persons in Process

rocess thought provides philosophical support for the
ious concept of soul. It is one of the few philosophical
ms that does so. What we think of as the traditional idea
ody and soul is a dualism which most philosophers today
t. There is good reason. If bodies and souls are two real
completely different kinds of substances, then there is no
for them to interact, to influence one another. Descartes,
devised such a dualistic system, had to appeal to the
nipotence of God for that interaction. Today many
osophers have accepted some form of materialism, in
h everything can be explained physically, and soul or con-
usness is conceived to be an "epiphenomenon" or
roduct of matter. Or they say that consciousness is a
ction" of the brain, or somewhat identical to it. They also
y dualism because there is no way to see how it could arise
physical atoms.[10]
Whitehead's view all individual entities are experiencing
ects. The things of this world are serially ordered occasions
xperience, each occasion occupying a tiny fraction of a sec-
. An occasion of experience is a creative synthesis of feelings
rior events. It comes together or happens all at once and
pies an indivisible unit of time.[11] This process is called a
ncrescence." However, it can be described as consisting of a

attribute of God from a philosophical point of view is "creativity"; from a theological point of view it is "love." These are the
implications of making love the divine essence.

Since God has a temporal aspect, and really is related to creation, the classical attributes of absolute knowledge (omni-
science) and absolute power (omnipotence) need modification.
God knows everything there is to be known. This includes perfect knowledge of all that has happened, as it really happened,
and knowledge of the future as it really is, uncertain, and not
yet determined. As many philosophers today insist, if things in
the future are really determined in the mind of God, then creatures are not really free. But that would be contrary to Christian
revelation, which insists that we have free will and are responsible for what we do.

Another aspect of the divine is its all-inclusive nature. If God
were to exist alone and then creatures were created outside
God, as classical theism asserts, then God plus creatures would
be a greater reality than God. Classical theism attempted to
explain this by saying that God contained all the value of what
was created, so the combination was not really greater.
However, no one has ever been able to explain how this could
be so. Rather, it seems clear that if God has all the value, then
creatures are really worthless, and life has no meaning. This
whole idea makes the criteria of God's nature as love a mock-
ery, for God could not love beings with no value.

Neoclassical theism holds that all created entities are "in"
God and influence each other. Hartshorne envisioned all physical entities as organisms, with some level of mentality, in every
created level, from the simplest elements to human beings. He
did not mean that atoms and cells are conscious or have minds.
Rather they have some level of subjectivity, reacting to the presence of others. Even atoms adjust their structure when emitting
or absorbing other particles. As the complexity of physical
arrangements goes up from molecules to cells, the level of mentality or subjectivity goes up, bringing into being creatures with

new levels of capability. One can think of these levels as the presence of some small amount of soul in all created things. This is an idea also proposed by Teilhard de Chardin. He called it the law of complexity-consciousness. The more complex the physical structure of a being becomes, he said, the greater becomes the level of that which in humans we call consciousness.[8]

We have been talking here about God's nature in a proposed theology of evolution. We want to address now how God works in creation, but for that we first need to discuss one important divine attribute neglected so far. It is time to talk about God's power. In classical theism, God had a monopoly on real power. God was omnipotent, meaning God can do anything not logically impossible. Creatures were allowed by God to exercise some power which could be withdrawn at any time. The problem with this was that if God had all the real power, God was responsible for evil, since if God could do anything and did not want evil, it wouldn't be there. Moral evil could always be explained as the result of human sin. But the problem was natural or physical evil, the application of sickness, natural disasters, pain and suffering to the innocent, with which, as we all know, the world is filled. Classical theism claimed that all the natural evil we observe was a necessary side-effect in a world of free human beings. Based upon the vast amounts of natural evil, and the classical concept of omnipotence, which held that God could do anything unilaterally, few theologians and philosophers today will buy that argument.

Absolute power is not a trait consistent with a God who *is* love; shared power is. A little reflection about love makes clear that there is nothing worthwhile that can occur between lovers that is coerced. In our neoclassical model, God's power is solely persuasive. God persuades creatures into being, granting them some power of creativity, but not just because God decides it would be nice to do so. It is the divine nature to create, because it is the divine nature to love. Love must share, love requires others. And, as Thomas Aquinas said, nothing

can act contrary to its nature.[9] As a result, God
the power in the universe. It is shared by cre
has all the power that a God could have who
with creatures who are really free.

It was the philosopher Whitehead who deve
tion of experience that explains how God an
together in the neoclassical model. He suggest
entities are made up of drops of experience, ar
itself, life itself for us humans, is an ordered se
brief occasions of experience. Thus, for hum
times a second, we constitute ourselves by me
(largely unconscious) concerning how and v
That we will exist is totally due to God; *how*
determined by our own God-given creativity,
God, our past, and the rest of the universe. T
occurs for all entities, from the basic particles of
to animals, to humans, and even to divinity itse

But how does an occasion of experience co
biggest factor determining what we will be in
of our existence is our past. Whitehead says w
as an agent causing our present. What we
instant must conform in large measure to wl
instant before. In addition, we must conform
to the influences upon us, influences we feel
around us. Finally, we feel God persuading
achieve some value held out to us as possibility
to accept God's invitation; we may reject it, o
partially. The decision is ours, and the decisior
we are.

With that little bit of subjectivity, that men
by every entity in the universe, God's creatu
selves what they are, and so participate in th
ture. From atoms to microbes to chimpanzee
their freedom as co-creators of God's univ
divine perspective, God feels the world, tal

number of phases. It is called into actuality by God who shares with it an element of divine creativity and provides it with a physical standpoint and an initial aim. This aim is a graded spectrum of possibilities for how the occasion can form itself. The becoming subject feels its past occasions and it feels its surroundings, the rest of the universe, in varying degrees.[12] During this process the occasion is a subject. It pulls its feelings together into a subjective aim and becomes concrete, enjoying a brief period of what Whitehead calls "satisfaction." In doing so it exercises the creativity given to it; it is self-creative to this extent. This subjectivity is an attribute of all actual occasions whether they are electrons, or the dominant occasions of consciousness in the human brain, the mind or soul. The subject then perishes and becomes an object, which means it exerts causal influence on the next occasion during its concrescence. The perished occasion is taken into the next occasion of the divine life, which felt it as it became actual. The pasts of all occasions are taken into the being of God where they are preserved everlastingly. Thus the divine nature is inclusive as we described earlier; the universe as it becomes actual is felt by God, and in an analogous sense becomes the body of God.

The divine call is toward complexity and consciousness. The various entities of nature that have evolved can be described as organisms. As they become more complex there have arisen dominant occasions that act for the whole. Thus, atoms, cells and animals can respond as a single unit. Other things in our world do not do so—for example, a rock or chair. These, in the neoclassical view are "aggregates" without a dominant occasion.[13] There is no central acting occasion in a crystal; the individual atom is the highest ranking being present. Other entities such as plants have some higher level occasions that allow motion and some coordinated activity.

The dominant occasions of the human mind are largely unconscious. The mind controls our breathing, our bodily functions, and most of what goes on within us without our being consciously aware of it. The psychologists have stressed how extensive and important the unconscious mind is for our very existence. What then is consciousness?

Consciousness, process theologian David Griffin tells us, is "the subjective form of an intellectual feeling, which arises, if at all, only in a late phase of a moment of experience."[14] Consciousness, said Whitehead, is "the crown of experience, only occasionally attained, not its necessary base." "Consciousness presupposes experience, and not experience consciousness," he tells us.[15]

Should we use the word "soul" for the mind or for consciousness? The actual thing in the brain, the concrescence, that which becomes an actuality, is a dominant occasion of experience. A serially ordered string or society of these occasions is the mind. Occasionally that mind is conscious. Consciousness is a state of the mind. But the mind, conscious or unconscious, is not a substance; it is a string of experiences. The word "soul" is a product of dualism; it presupposes a spiritual substance inserted into a body, so we need to redefine it. More than that, we need to begin thinking about it in a new way.

Minds and consciousness are not limited to human beings: animals are conscious. Some of the higher animals, such as chimpanzees, are even self-conscious. They have memory and anticipation, can plan for the future, and are aware of themselves. What we have called subjectivity, or mentality, is present in all individual creatures, from atoms to cells to animals, in varying degrees. Mentality, or what we previously meant by soul in humans, is a matter of degree. In the evolution of more complex entities the mind developed to serve the body, coordinating its activities, for the body's enjoyment. As the mind developed the ability to transcend the needs of the body, and developed continuity of control, a shift occurred, and the mind began to control the body for its own purposes. At this point perhaps we could speak of an "animal soul," although traditionally we have restricted use of that term to our own species.[16] In any case, in the process worldview, mind has evolved in steps just as have animal bodies. There is no substance that has been placed into the human body that can be marked, or that is different in kind from animal souls. The difference is in degree, but that difference in the case of a mature, rational human being, capable of transcending the world in loving response to God, is immense.

We have been building up to the very difficult subject of the human person. Defining "personhood" is extremely difficult. Philosophers today have no agreed-upon definition.[17] Moral theologians offer various opinions as they struggle to deal with such problems as abortion and euthanasia, where the concept of personhood is critical. We are not going to solve this huge question here, but we will offer a few suggestions coming from the process model.

The definition of personhood in moral questions is related to rights, the rights of the person. Rights in turn are related to duties. If I have the right to life and freedom, you have the duty not to kill or enslave me. We must consider then with what species, and when in an individual's development, these rights and duties come into play. That which we call soul in humans is not a substance that appears at conception or birth. The potential to become a human being occurs at conception. But the potential is not the actual; therefore the becoming of a human being goes through many stages in time. Personhood develops in time. The mature human is self-conscious, has memories, hopes and fears, anticipates the future, and transcends the physical world in value, creativity, and knowledge of God. The development of human personhood has direct implications for moral decisions. Since personhood goes through stages as a human matures, it is not an absolute, and cannot be used as though it were, to support arguments against abortion or euthanasia, for example.[18]

The process viewpoint even has implications for animal

rights. Since all individuals, human and otherwise, are felt by God, and thus have value in themselves, they have rights and we have duties toward them. The reasons for not killing humans can be seen to extend naturally to some of the higher animals. Killing a human brings to an end a series of personal, creative experiences of value. Fear of death diminishes the joy of life and the value of living, and the death of an individual brings pain and suffering to other lives. These same factors, it can be argued, apply in varying degrees to animals.[19] Dolphins and chimps are self-aware, experience fear, and mourn the lose of family and friends. Don't we have the duty to see that such creatures are not tortured and killed?

Another theological implication of the neoclassical view of person is in the area of eschatology, particularly survival after death. While various process thinkers have disagreed about the likelihood of personal immortality, they all agree that such immortality is not ruled out by the process worldview. If immortality is affirmed, as Christians do affirm it, on the basis of the Resurrection and the divine promise, then the process worldview can provide various insights into such questions as judgment, heaven and hell. We pointed out earlier that individual experiences occur in little units of time, and that as each one reaches completion or satisfaction it is taken into the divine life. The divine life is constantly receiving the lives of everyone in the world, and adding each moment to all the collected moments of their past. All these moments are experienced in God with no loss of intensity or immediacy. The past of the world enters the everlasting present of the divine immediacy. The world is transformed in God, who weaves everything that is worthwhile into a greater harmony, a greater whole. Evils are dismissed into the triviality of individual facts, reduced to insignificance in terms of the divine harmony.

While such a transformation is beyond our imagination to conceive, proposals have been made. Process theologian Marjorie Suchocki has made splendid suggestions in this regard.[20] She suggests that individuals are reborn in God's everlasting concrescence. They experience a dual consciousness, seeing things from their own and from God's point of view. They are united to God, participants in the divine becoming, experiencing God's transformation of themselves and of the world. Each entity is saved by its relation to the completed whole. All times are present. In God, she suggests, finite personal identity is "thick." When a person sees his or her life and the world from the divine point of view, this is judgment, and in accord with the value in that life could be experienced with joy (heaven), or as purgative suffering. In Suchocki's vision, universal redemption is required by this eschatology. Evil is overcome, as each individual moves from full understanding of the effects of its own life through a purgative transformation into the divine life.[21]

Evolution in Neoclassical Perspective

Evolution is the result of factors that involve both chance and purpose. Although both God and creatures are involved, the outcome cannot be predicted exactly either by creatures or by divinity itself. An example may help us to understand.

Consider an evolutionary change which makes some fruit flies become resistant to the insecticide DDT. That this occurs is due to an interplay of purpose and chance. Let us review how it happens, using the neoclassical model. A mutation due to cosmic radiation occurs in one gene located on the DNA of a certain type of fruit fly. This is a matter of chance. Most mutations are harmful to an organism, but this one makes the fly resistant to DDT, and it breeds. That this occurs at some particular time and place is also a matter of chance. Now, humans have introduced DDT into the area occupied by the flies with this gene change. This was a matter of human purpose. The fact that both humans and flies are there, and pursuing their own aims, which are responsive in varying degrees to divine lures, is due to divine purpose and the purposes of the creatures involved. So what happens?

All the flies in the area are exposed to the DDT. Most are killed off, but not the few resistant to the DDT. Now they breed without competition, and the new flies are all resistant to the pesticide. Did any one entity make this happen? Are the flies, or the humans, or even God totally responsible for this happening? No, God was responsible for the existence of all, and for luring them to live and evolve toward value. But the creatures were free to exercise various degrees of self-determination. Both purpose and chance were involved. Physicist-philosopher of science Ian Barbour has summed up the process well.

> Chance is present at many levels: mutations, genetic recombinations, genetic drift, climactic variations, and so forth. Evolution is an unrepeatable series of events that no one could have predicted; it can only be described historically. Yet history has seen an ascent to higher levels of organization, a trend toward greater organization and sentience. The dice are thrown, but the dice are loaded; there are built-in constraints...so the advances are conserved.[22]

Thus, there is a general direction for evolution in accord with divine aims. But there is no detailed pre-ordained plan for our existence, because our response, and that of all God's creatures, cannot be coerced or exactly predicted.[23]

So, God has been working for billions of years to bring the universe in the desired direction. But since all creatures really have some measure of self-creativity, they have responded only imperfectly. They partially share with God the directions evolution has taken. God can only suggest the way evolution should go, and then must experience with creatures the results of the decisions that they make. This explains the vast quantities of time necessary to see any sizable creative advance. It also explains the tremendous diversity of life as each creature goes its own way. It explains the blind alleys and the dead ends of evolutionary advance. It is all due to finite self-creating creatures freely responding to the lure of God, each in its own way. It is only during the last century that we are coming to understand what has been going on. We are learning the universe's story, a story in which we share. We are becoming aware of who we are and of our relationship with God within the divine creation. Considering what has just been said about the role of creatures in evolution, it seems amazing that there has been any advance at all. That advance is due to God.

Rather than being unneeded in the process of evolution, the presence of God is absolutely essential. Order requires an orderer. Chance alone is incapable of producing a creative advance to higher levels of being. Our universe requires the laws of nature, and as Charles Hartshorne reminds us, "That there are laws of nature is providential."[24] The laws of nature are the democratic response to the lure of God addressed to the fundamental particles of the universe. Indeed, they have very little subjectivity and thus very little capability to respond; therefore action took eons of time. As they began to respond they felt their past as determinative of the present, and they felt each other in vast numbers all moving in the same direction. Since God is the most powerful entity in the universe, divinity is felt with the greatest clarity by fundamental entities, and their democratic response becomes the laws of nature. We say "democratic" because, as in a democratic society, the individual has some power of self-determination but is limited by the mutually agreed-upon order established by the masses under the direction of a leader. The laws of nature are produced in the same way by the individual response of the fundamental constituents of the universe to the persuasive power of God.

The existence of some measure of self-determination necessitates the tremendous amounts of time involved in the evolutionary process, and the tiny statistical variations in physical laws

are described by quantum theory. Not every fundamental parti-
cle of physics responds in exactly the same way, and that is a
demonstrated fact.[25]

Since the universe is "in" God, and felt by God as we feel
our bodies, our lives have real value because we contribute to
the divine life. Evidently, God's purpose is to create value,
goodness and beauty. Evolution is God enjoying creatures.

Evil Revisited

What about evil? Moral evil, or sin, is produced by evil
wills. But we said that a God who had all the real power, as in
classical theism, was ultimately and morally responsible for
natural evil and the suffering of the innocent. What about in
our modified "neoclassical" theism? Let's look at how evil in
nature occurs. Consider some terrible natural disaster, say
some volcanic eruption that buries people alive. It is a chance
occurrence resulting from the partial response of created entities over billions of years. The interior of the earth cools,
molten magma plumes churn in the earth's interior and plates
shift position on the surface. In some places there is plate sub-
duction where the crust is forced down under an adjacent
plate, heating the material and pushing up mountain ranges.
Hot spots form underneath and chains of volcanic activity
occur sporadically. God is powerless to stop an eruption.
There is no controlling entity in a volcano as a whole that
could respond to divine persuasion. Chance and order result
in both creative advance and in disasters.

Yet there is a sense in which God is responsible. If God's
nature was not love which required the creation of others,
the disaster would not have occurred, because the universe
would not exist. But, in this model, it is the divine nature to
love and create, and impossible for divinity to do otherwise.
Therefore God is not morally responsible for the suffering

that occasionally occurs. God does not will the suffering; just the opposite, God feels the suffering, all of it, with greater intensity than is humanly possible. Thus, God is physically responsible for evil, but not morally indictable for it.

Some physical evil is also produced by created entities. Since all created beings have some measure of self-determination, they can compete for survival. The good of one often results in harmful results upon another. For beings with levels of mentality below consciousness, the individuals harming others cannot be held morally responsible. With consciousness comes moral responsibility and sin. The race's moral "fall" followed its elevation to rational consciousness.[26]

Realizing that God's power is only persuasive is mentally wrenching for some Christians who derive a great sense of comfort from the idea that God's providential power means that God can jump in and save them from any possible situation, if only God wills to do so. The common human experience that God does not jump in and save people from natural disasters, or things like airplane crashes, has to be explained away as inexplicable divine judgment, or action designed to educate us spiritually, or some other reason. Rather, the realization that God's power is persuasive suggests that action to overcome natural evil must come from our action as God's partners, responding to God's grace-filled urging. God can't persuade a cancer cell from establishing itself and growing in a critical site in a human body, because such response is not a possibility for such a cell. God can persuade a doctor to take an action to kill or remove such a cell, resulting in preservation of human life.

We really don't know the limits of God's persuasive power. It may be much greater than we imagine. Current scientific work on non-linear chaotic systems suggests that very tiny initial impulses can produce massive effects. It's the "beat of the wing of the butterfly" idea—namely, that under the right circumstances it is capable of producing a hurricane on the other side of the world. The divine lures, guided by divinity's perfect knowledge of the world, may be capable on occasion of producing massive results. In any case, the neoclassical view of God makes more understandable the pervasive presence of natural evil that we see in the world, even though that world is created by a God who is love.

The Universe's Clues and the Divine Nature

It should be apparent by now that the clues present in our new knowledge of the universe are a better fit with a neoclassical model for God than with a classical one. No doubt as we grow more knowledgeable, these concepts too will be superseded by still better models.

The tremendous amount of time it took for the simplest elements of matter to form themselves into stars, and to make the other elements, is consistent with the concepts of persuasive power and minimal creaturely response. A God with classical omnipotent power who could create anything at a word, would not produce the universe as we know it today. The messy aspects of evolution, the diversity of life bursting into all niches available after extinctions, the dead ends of evolution, dinosaurs in vast array living for hundreds of millions of years, the parasites, the disease bacteria, nature "red in tooth and claw"—all these things become more understandable in the light of a persuasive God and co-creating creatures. The evolving universe makes no sense whatsoever if divinity has the characteristics of classical theism. No wonder the idea of evolution is so repugnant to biblical literalists.

In the neoclassical model all beings have some measure of subjectivity, and are in continual interaction with God as they move forward in time as a series of events, like drops of time. Therefore, the inhabitants of the universe do not consist of objects for human use and exploitation. They are creatures as we are, and their existence, their lives, give value to God. Since this relatedness exists, we have some measure of responsibility toward each other. Most beings are societies of lesser beings: atoms made up of nuclear particles, cells of macro-molecules, animals of many types of cells. All are organisms, and may be described as ecologies, where many parts are interrelated and necessary for mutual survival. This calls for a theology that is ecologically sensitive, a theology that is aware that we are partners in God's universe and must be concerned for the whole. As the dominant and most conscious species on earth we find ourselves in the position of caretakers of the garden earth. This reminds us of many things said in the book of Genesis, doesn't it? Now, this worldview can assist us in proper interpretation of Genesis and the other books of the Bible. Thomas Berry, a Passionist priest and follower of Teilhard de Chardin, has summarized well what some of these clues from the universe tell us.

> The universe as such is the primary religious reality, the primary sacred community, the primary revelation of the divine, the primary subject of incarnation, the primary unit of redemption, the primary referent in any discussion of reality or of value.[27]

The neoclassical model proposes that God feels the universe, and that the value of each created creature is a value in the divine life. Not only does this mean that all creatures really are valuable, it means that the enjoyment of creatures is the purpose of the universe. The universe exists for the enjoyment of God, not just to show forth God's glory, as the classical model suggests. Of course, it does show God's glory; but rather than just paying a metaphysical compliment to a God who couldn't care less, now in the neoclassical model the loving relationship between divinity and creatures is real and produces shared joy.

Further, in the neoclassical worldview, there is nothing to suggest the immediate arrival of the eschaton, the second coming of Christ. Divinity may indeed be calling the human race forward to a consummation far beyond our ability to understand, but our current understanding of how God works in the world suggests that anything of that sort will be far in the future. We must be responsible for not destroying ourselves by making the earth unable to sustain life.

Finally, in this new model, there is no room for any kind of anthropocentrism. The biblical stories were written by people for whom the cosmos consisted of humans on earth, God and his angels above, and the devil below. The universe's story shows that we are minute specks on a planet orbiting a medium-size star, two-thirds of the way out on a spiral arm of a galaxy consisting of a hundred million stars, and among billions of such galaxies. In all probability, God has called into existence races of intelligent beings long before humanity evolved, and will continue to do so forever. Our God has been too small, and the divine kingdom and interests are more vast than we can imagine. Our theology must begin to reflect this. This situation in no way depreciates our relationship with God, although it perhaps hurts our pride and feelings of self-importance.

A theology of evolution is part of a fundamental theology. That is, it concerns the nature of God, and the divine relationship with creatures. We have been talking here about the nature of divinity and how God works in the world, based on a neoclassical model. The other main subject of fundamental theology is that of "revelation." Revelation in a neoclassical model can be viewed as a process of interpersonal communion with God.[28]

This follows from the Vatican II presentation of revelation as human experience of God. From both Whitehead's metaphysics and modern Catholic theology, we can conclude that religious experience, like all experience, is mediated symbolically. Following our neoclassical view of how God works with creatures, providing lures to value, revelation is seen as stemming from those lures of God continually impinging upon the soul. When individuals align their own aims and purposes to be in accord with those proposed by God, there is a resonance effect in which the presence of God is magnified and consciously felt. It is like tuning-in a television set. When the frequency of reception matches exactly the incoming signal, the message is received clearly. The human efforts of those inspired members of the early Church to witness to their experience of revelation produced the Scriptures and and the traditions of the Church.[29]

What remains to be done in Catholic theology is to apply the insights of a neoclassical fundamental theology to dogmatic theology. Dogmatic theology based upon Scripture, but informed by either a classical Greek worldview or by some unconscious metaphysical presuppositions (by those who don't want to use metaphysics at all in theology), has produced results that are in opposition to modern science and philosophy. In much of theology this has not had disastrous effects on the Christian message. But in areas which impinge upon scientific knowledge, it has produced results that are not credible. We have spoken of some of these results earlier in our discussion of evolution. In the next chapter we will take the first step and apply the neoclassical model to the human situation before God, and the implication of that situation for human destiny. We will consider "original sin."

6
Original Sin and the Future of Catholic Doctrine

> The harm that has been done to souls, during the centuries of Christianity, first by the literal interpretation of the story of Adam, and then by the confusion of this myth, treated as history, with later speculations, principally Augustinian, about original sin, will never be adequately told. In asking the faithful to confess belief in this mythico-speculative mass and to accept it as a self-sufficient explanation, the theologians have unduly required a *sacrificium intellectus* where what was needed was to awaken believers to a symbolic superintelligence of their actual condition.—Paul Ricoeur[1]

Ricoeur is right on the money with his remarks, but we would not want anyone to misunderstand him. He is not suggesting that there is no such thing as "original sin." Nor is he taking a Pelagian position that humanity by its own efforts alone can perfect itself. Note that last phrase in the quotation, "their actual condition." And what is that condition? Another quote, this time from Protestant theologian Reinhold Niebuhr, answers the question well. "The view that men are 'sinful' is one of the best attested and empirically verified facts of human existence."[2] Niebuhr also is right on target. If there is one thing that should be clear to us today, it is that human beings are sinners. Our century has been filled with war, genocide and terrorism, the pervasive presence of human sin and evil. It is not something that any amount of education and effort on the part of humanity alone can overcome. What is popularly called "original sin" is indeed real. Here I hope to frame an interpretation of original sin in the light of our understanding of human evolution, and in the light of current scriptural and theological understanding.

Theologians, consciously or unconsciously, work from a base of fundamental theology that deals with the nature of God, and God's creatures, and how they interrelate, in addition to drawing their inspiration from Scripture and the life of the Church. I have sketched a neoclassical framework for fundamental theology based on the revelation that God *is* love. It harmonized with clues about the divine nature inferred from the story of the universe. It is the job of dogmatic theologians to reinterpret Christian doctrines for their own age in the light of the best fundamental theology available. I will attempt to show how this can be done for the case of "original sin." In the words of philosopher Paul Ricoeur, we need to see and hear anew the divine manifestation and message in the myths of origin, through reinterpretation. We need, as modern Christians, to aim at "a second naïveté, in and through criticism."[3] Then, in the light of our reexamination, we will experience that "the symbol gives rise to the thought."[4]

In the second chapter it was noted that the official Catholic position on original sin, as given in *Catechism of the Catholic Church,* has come down to us from Augustine by way of the Council of Trent. It assumes an historical understanding of the story of Adam and Eve, and posits a universe created at once out of nothing, and human beings created in a graced state, not subject to suffering and death. It proposes that their rebellion against God was a crime so horrible that divine justice demanded punishment not only of the first couple, but of all their descendants. As a result, nature itself was changed for the worse, and humanity became deserving of death in this life, and, unless saved by God's grace, deserving of eternal damnation.

We noted how Augustine, sensitive to the massive amount of physical evil in the world, which results in the suffering of the innocent, found the reason for evil in divine punishment. It must be punishment, he reasoned, because an all-powerful and good God would not allow such suffering unless it was warranted. Searching Scripture for the reason for such punishment, Augustine found it in Adam's sin. Thus, God was spared responsibility for physical evil, sin and death.

As a result of the fall, human wills were weakened and became subject to concupiscence, the inherited inclination to evil, which Augustine largely equated with lust. The human body was no longer controlled completely by reason, but became subject to control by the flesh. Human guilt was passed on by sexual generation. Baptism removes the state of original sin; concupiscence remains.

In Chapter 3 we reviewed the theological advances of Vatican II concerning the nature of revelation. We saw that modern Scripture studies, officially supported by that council and the Church hierarchy today, accept the non-historical nature of Genesis 1–11. And we reviewed a variety of theological studies on original sin which see the doctrine as compatible with an evolutionary point of view. But many of the modern treatments are still hampered by the perceived need to find some mysterious way to show that original sin is a distinct reality for which humans are responsible, that changed the world, and resulted in the observed surfeit of physical evil.

We want to propose a new viewpoint on original sin. Therefore, we need to correlate two things: our human biological and cultural inheritance revealed in studies of human evolution, and a fundamental theology that can throw light on the problem of evil. Such a theology grows out of the realization that the power of a God who *is* love is persuasive. This realization is supported by a neoclassical worldview such as the one we discussed in the last chapter. These elements need to be combined in creative fidelity to the meaning of the doctrine of original sin which our understandings of Scripture and revelation have provided.

Our Evolutionary Heritage

We are concerned here with the evolution of human self-consciousness before God. If sin is rebellion against God, it requires recognition of the self in the divine presence, recognition of self under the dictates of conscience, and freedom of self-determination. How and when did these things arise in our evolutionary history? These are difficult questions, and exact answers are not available. However, the broad outline of the process and possible scenarios are obtainable, just as the broad outline of the universe's story, described in Chapter 4, is known.

The key to understanding our heritage is in the observed buildup of complexity in the central nervous systems of the organisms from which we evolved. Life came out of the sea and learned to live on the land. The creatures of the sea gave rise to reptiles, and then to mammals. Fins became limbs for movement on land, lungs adapted to take oxygen directly from the air. At each step in the chain of evolving organisms there occurred modifications of what was previously there. Evolution did not start over at each step up the chain of complexity-consciousness. There was a building upon what existed previously. We can see this mirrored today in the development of a human embryo. At an early stage the embryo has gills, which are of no use to a fetus nourished by an umbilical cord. The embryo then passes through stages that appear very much like reptiles, and then non-primate mammals, before becoming recognizably human. Evolution works on what was there before. As long as the presence of gills causes no problem for human fetuses and are lost before birth, they can be retained. There is no process for their removal because natural selection, the weeding out of those unfit for their environment, acts mostly on individuals, not on fetuses or eggs. The latest evolutionary adaption then appears at birth. Evolution by addition, and the retention of preexisting features, occurs either because the old function is required in addition to the new, or because there is no way of bypassing the old system that is consistent for survival.[5]

This recapitulation of evolutionary forms is especially instructive in the case of the formation of the human brain. There are layers of the brain built up around the spinal cord— first the hindbrain and mid-brain which together are called the "neural chassis."[6] This chassis regulates reproduction and self-preservation, including blood circulation and respiration. The chassis is then surrounded successively by three layers, the reptilian complex, the limbic system and the neocortex. The reptilian complex probably evolved several hundred million years ago. Medical researcher Dr. Paul MacLean has shown that in lizards it is involved in the daily routine, and for displays related to aggressiveness, courtship, and other social behavior.[7] All these behaviors may be characterized as instinctive.

The limbic system probably evolved about 150 million years ago; we share it with mammals and the higher primates. It has been shown to play a role in the experience and expression of emotions.[8] One part of the limbic system is involved in sexual functions and behavior. In recent years, another part has been found to be the neural substrate for family-related functions such as nursing and maternal care, vocal communication to maintain contact between mothers and offspring, and playful behavior.

The neocortex is the site of many human cognitive functions: deliberation and regulation of action, spatial perception, vision, anticipation and worry.[9] While it is true that the triune brain is an oversimplification as regards separation of function—emotional behavior is also influenced by reasoning in the neocortex—still it reveals the amounts of instinctive or unconscious behavior controlled by regions of the brain not open to our internal self-inspection. Much of what we do in our daily lives is controlled by the unconscious mind. Psychologists, such as Carl Jung, have pleaded for recognition of the importance of understanding our unconscious minds, so that human rationality can gain control of our culture.[10]

But our heritage is not just biological, it is also cultural, and the interplay and relative importance of these two areas in determining human behavior are hotly contested. The contest is the battle between nature and nurture. In recent years the new subject of "sociobiology" has appeared upon the scene. The sociobiologists are convinced that a great deal of human behavior is genetically determined, or at least strongly influenced by the genes.[11] While it is certainly true that at least a predisposition toward many types of behavior is genetically determined, so far no specific behavior has been reduced to the characteristics of one specific gene. Most human behavior is thought to involve many genes. Representative of the culture or nurture side of the argument is social anthropologist, and editor for many years of the journal *Current Anthropology,* Adam Kuper.[12] While the biologists would prefer a primate model for humanity, says Kuper, "The other party...does not, of course, deny the common primate ancestry of humanity, but it points out that our primate origins did not determine the particular course taken by human evolution....Culture is a uniquely human achievement, and it is simply perverse to deny the distinctiveness and significance of the cultural factor in human history."[13] For a number of years there was considerable discussion about human aggressive traits. The results were conflicting. Robert Ardrey wrote of humans as descended from killer apes. A. Alland, and Richard Leakey and Roger Lewin saw our hunter-gatherer ancestors as quite non-violent.[14] It would appear that under appropriate circumstances humans can act either way. A number of studies on evolution and culture were reviewed by biologist Charles Birch and theologian John Cobb.[15] They concluded that the studies had not advanced sufficiently as yet for us to be sure how much human behavior is related to our biology, and how much to culture.

> We just do not know enough about complex behavioral traits of humans to be able to say with any confidence the extent to which genetic and cultural components are involved....For the present, however, the reliable results of the sociobiology debate are rather small....It seems clear that the genetic constitution sets constraints on behavior but that within those constraints culture has a decisive influence on what people do and do not do.[16]

Just when did human self-consciousness appear in the course of evolution? Again, this is not exactly known. The brain size of our ancestors began to increase dramatically, without corresponding increases in body mass, about two million years ago. *Archaic Homo sapiens,* who appeared perhaps 400,000 years ago, had a brain size about double that of *Homo erectus,* who lived about 1.5 million years ago. These early *Homo sapiens* brains were as large as ours.[17] Brain size may not be enough to explain human intelligence, however. Internal organization and structure are also considered important. The development of language is thought to have had a strong influence on intellectual development.[18] There is evidence that earlier species in the *Homo* line created and used stone tools (1.5 million years ago), and there is evidence of the use of fire about 400,000 years ago.

The Neanderthals, who are not thought to be in our ancestral line, made beautiful stone tools of many types. They first appeared about 200,000 years ago, and disappeared about 35,000 years ago. They, at least occasionally, provided long-term care of the disabled and buried their dead.[19]

Modern *Homo sapiens,* our species, arrived on the scene

somewhere from 130,000 to 100,000 years ago. They probably arose in Africa, and were anatomically just like us.[20] Deliberate human burial is found around 100,000 years ago, which "suggests an awareness of the possibility of a future life and demonstrates the existence of formal ritual."[21] In the past forty to fifty thousand years we see the first shaped bone tools, representational art, and bone needles suggesting sewing. We are getting to the period in which, anthropologists have concluded, the people were humans just like us.

> The Aurignacians (40,000 years ago), the first modern culture group in Europe, left immediate evidence of art, notation, symbolism, music, sophisticated manipulation of materials, a restless spirit of innovation, and all of those basic behavioral elements that we associate with ourselves.[22]

While findings, such as sophisticated cave paintings, have led anthropologists to conclude that they were made by people just like us, their studies suggest that many human traits developed much earlier.

> All this reinforces the view that through the past 30,000 to 40,000 years the brains of modern *Homo sapiens* were similar to our own. Physical and cultural evidence points to lower levels of mental ability and craft skill in earlier periods. Nevertheless, we may have to concede that the foundations of many basic human skills were laid 1 or even 2 million years ago, rather than at the origins of our own species.[23]

The evidence available suggests that human beings capable of self-consciousness and recognition of a creator first existed between 40,000 and 100,000 years ago. As evidence continues to accumulate, these numbers may be pushed even further back into the past. The emergence of our kind was gradual. "Population genetics," as population geneticist Charles Birch tells us, shows us that "species can only be characterized by the means of characters and their variability.

What happens in evolution is not that the type suddenly changes but the mean of the population in many of its characters gradually moves."[24] Teilhard de Chardin made the point well.

> Man came silently into the world. As a matter of fact he trod so softly that, when we first catch sight of him as revealed by those indestructible stone instruments, we find him sprawling all over the old world from the Cape of Good Hope to Peking. Without doubt he already speaks and lives in groups; he already makes fire. After all, this is surely what we ought to expect. As we know, each time a new living form rises up before us out of the depths of history, it is always complete and already legion.
>
> Thus *in the eyes of science,* which at long range can only see things in bulk, the "first man" is, and can only be, a *crowd,* and his infancy is made up of thousands and thousands of years.[25]

Teilhard's conclusions have been supported by recent anthropological studies. A few years ago, a study of the DNA found in Mitochondria (the energy-producing sites in cells), which is inherited from the female line, suggested that all women today are descendants of an African Eve who lived over 50,000 years ago. A newer statistical study, however, disagreed with that conclusion. But even if that first study is supported, geneticists tell us that it can never be proven that there were not many other women around at the same time whose female lineage died out. In fact, they say several common ancestors appearing at different periods in history are likely statistically, and they probably had many other people living with them at the same time. An "Eve," they say, is only a statistical artifact.[26]

Original Sin Revisited

In light of what scientists can tell us about human origins, modern Catholic biblical scholars recognize that the origin stories in Genesis 1–11 are not meant to be understood as historical fact. Therefore, we need not take as literal truth that human beings began their existence in a paradise, and were endowed with beyond human capabilities of knowledge and bodily control, and were without suffering and death. And, most important of all, one need not conclude that there was an offense committed by the first human beings so horrible that the justice of God demanded that henceforth they and their descendants be punished with suffering and death, and declared guilty of eternal damnation. The nature of the universe was not changed as a result of this "fall," and physical evil was not henceforth inflicted by God upon the earth as punishment. Original sin was not some primal crime. As theologian Stephen Duffy reminds us, "It is the contradiction between what humans are and what they are called to become in Christ."[27]

What humans are is what we have just been considering. They are the product of fifteen billion years of the evolution of matter and a universe. They are the result of some four billion years of the evolution of life on planet earth. They are the result of the evolution of a long line of mammals, primates and hominids. They are evolution become conscious of itself. Humans carry within themselves the cumulative results of their past. They carry the traces and remnants that when modified allowed survival. The atoms that compose them were born in stars. The central nervous system that animates them was developed from simpler forms of animal life. They have arisen in response to the divine call from the dust of the earth and have found self-consciousness, freedom and God.

The human past is filled with the mutation and natural selection of finite entities. As one survived, another did not. Human beings survived because they were best at surviving. Humans are here today because their ancestors had a strong survival instinct. At times survival required resistance against other creatures, aggression and violence. Our ancient animal ancestors ate and were eaten by others. Human beings are still capable of these things as we know. For the millions of years during which human bodies, nervous systems, and brains were evolving, they developed instincts and traits that are now present in the genes, the central nervous system, and the many layers of the human brain. And most of this was done without self-consciousness. Our hominid ancestors were emotion-laden individuals long before they were self-conscious. Anger, fear, maternal love, sexual arousal, awe at nature and intimations of the creator—all these were present before sin. There was suffering and evil for millions of years, but no guilt, and no sin.

Our hominid ancestors developed hunter-gatherer cultures, some of whose characteristics can be inferred from the cultures of modern primates. Genes and cultures interact in ways as yet little understood. The selfishness of individuals at times conflicted with the altruism required to increase group survival. Such conflicts may have produced early forms of guilt.[28] Local groups set up their societies with structures designed to enhance their survival. Group behaviors and the training of individuals to follow these behaviors benefited the group to the detriment of others. The coming of self-consciousness was indeed a kind of "fall," as Birch and Cobb have suggested, a "fall upward,"[29] because before the realization of the self, standing before God, and hearing the divine call to transcend human inclinations, and the realization of the freedom to respond or resist, there was no sin.

Human beings come into the world carrying a lot of baggage. The kind of living to which they are predisposed by their genes and by their culture is not consistent with the kind of life to which they are called by Christ. In this sense, they *do* enter the world in a state of alienation from God. There *is* a state of original sin, but it might better be called a "sin of origin," because the state exists because we evolved.[30] Original sin is the biologically and culturally inherited state, responsible for the human characteristics of survival and self-interest, which has resulted from fifteen billion years of persuasive divine creativity and the co-creative response of all entities of our universe. Humans are born into this state, but are not actually sinners until they knowingly defy the divine call. The divine call to each individual is a call to transcend his or her predispositions, instincts, and social training. Because one is born into the world in this state, as an evolved human being, one is predisposed to evil. Thus, concupiscence also is real, and is our natural inheritance, not the presence of the devil making the flesh lust against the spirit. Concupiscence, in this explanation, precedes sin.

If the state of alienation, the state of "original sin," is the result of God's creation by evolution, rather than an ancestral wrong justifying natural evil as punishment from a just God, then what is the source of the massive amounts of natural evil? As we saw in the last chapter, a neoclassical worldview, which posits a divine nature that has as its essence love and creativity, is consistent with the gospels and with the clues from the universe. Our God of persuasive power calls into existence creatures who have some power of self-determination. Because these created, evolving entities are finite and what is good for one often means a bad result for others, and because these creatures resist the divine call and seek selfish ends, natural evil is produced. Some beings survive, others do not. Evolved human beings are the joint product of the divine call and creaturely response. God is *responsible* for natural evil, because there would be no creatures without God; but God is not *indictable* for evil, because God does not will it. It happens because love and creativity *are* the divine nature; God and self-determining creatures to love go together. Natural evil cannot be overcome immediately by the power of a God who *is* love; it will take time. But it is our Christian faith that "he shall overcome."

In light of the above, then, we can focus on the abundance of God's grace as the real meaning of Genesis 1–11. St. Paul was talking about the same abundant grace when he set up the parallel between Adam in the Genesis story and the grace of Jesus Christ.

> If, because of the one man's trespass, death exercised domin-ion through that one, much more surely will those who receive the abundance of grace and the free gift of righteous-ness exercise dominion in life through the one man, Jesus Christ (Romans 5:17).

In chapter 3, we repeated the formulation of theologian Gabriel Daly, "The core of the doctrine traditionally labeled 'original sin' is the assertion that to be human is to need redemption."[31] Human beings come into the world as evolved creatures with inherited predispositions toward selfish behav-ior. As Reinhold Niebuhr also said, "It (original sin) means merely that the capacity and inclination of the self to give its interests undue regard can arise on every level of culture and moral attainment."[32] To become a child of God requires tran-scending one's own selfishness, and this requires the grace of Christ which, happily, is available to all as divine gift. That is the "good news."

In the light of the reinterpretation of "original sin" pro-posed in this chapter, the concerns originally voiced in Pope Pius XII's *Humani Generis* are no longer problems. There is no need to insist on direct creation of each human soul by God. God is continually active in creation of each event of the universe at all times, and the physical and mental aspects of creatures evolve together. Human dignity is based on the common call to become sons and daughters of God, destined to union with Divinity, not on possession of a substance called soul. In our neoclassical worldview, all creatures con-tain some measure of subjectivity, which in advanced beings we call mentality, and in humans we call soul. The difference between the subjectivity of primates and humans is much less than once thought. It is a matter of degree rather than of kind. In this sense, all individual creatures have some measure of soul.

There is also no need to insist that all humans can be traced back directly through sexual generation to Adam and Eve to insure that all require redemption. The human race is united by its destiny in Jesus Christ, not by direct descent from Adam. All humans require the grace of God because they *are* human, the product of an evolving, self-seeking universe. We don't need the terrible sin of a first parent to practically guarantee that we will sin.

The human need for redemption, salvation, or atonement through Jesus Christ is necessary because of what we are, selfish by nature and nurture. The sins of the world flow from our genetic heritage which has evolved in a struggle for survival, from human relationships that seek the security of the local group, and from human institutions designed to stabilize power for the interests of their founders.

This revitalized view of original sin has implications for the meaning of redemption and atonement. There has never been a direct ecclesial or conciliar definition of redemption. New Testament references to redemption spell out its meaning in a myriad of images and symbols. Redemption is achieved through the life, death, and resurrection of Jesus Christ, and yet remains to be achieved.[33] In apostolic and medieval times many different theories were worked out. The meaning of Jesus' death and resurrection were seen as sacrifice, as vicarious satisfaction for our sins, as ransom paid to the devil, and as victory over sin and death. For others, Jesus merited our redemption by the superabundance of his love, and by revealing God's love for us by his teaching and example. The reformers stressed the substitutional role of Jesus who underwent the penal suffering that we deserved for our sins. Karl Rahner emphasizes God's universal salvific will. For him, Jesus' death and resurrection are symbols that cause what they signify, our salvation.[34]

Clearly many symbols are necessary here since redemption has to be both personal and universal, both political and inclusive. Redemption as eschatology involves both the Christian community and the universe. But, it appears that some traditional theories, such as those of redemption as sacrifice, ransom to the devil, satisfaction for God's honor, and perhaps penal suffering, are not very meaningful considering our understanding of the human condition today. The "classic" theory of atonement, the early patristic concept of our salvation being achieved by Christ's victory over our enemies, sin and death, which resulted in our immortality, still makes good sense. Christ has shown us the way, and provided the means to overcome both sin and the sting of death. However, it is beyond the scope of our considerations here to attack this huge subject. It is the task of the dogmatic theologians to apply the results of fundamental theology's proposals on the divine nature and humanity's place and condition to the Church's formulations.

The Evolution of Doctrine

It is hoped that we have shown how the coming together of scientific knowledge with modern theological advances and a credible worldview can enlighten our understanding of our faith, and provide it with support. We have spoken of a theology of evolution, by which we mean not only a theology enlightened by encounter with knowledge of evolution, but one that will assist humanity in dealing with its future. You may recall, however, that back when we were discussing biological evolution, we noted that continued human evolution was on hold because the conditions for it were not right. Evolution requires that parts of the species be subjected to quite different environments; but as the earth's population increases, human life is becoming more densely packed and intermixed. It will probably require space travel and clusters of humans living in the weightlessness of space, or other significantly different gravitational fields, to accelerate the evolutionary process again.

We would like to suggest, however, that a theology of evolution may have significant benefits for humanity's future as it evolves culturally and historically, and faces new problems. Perhaps we could speculate on one possibility as an example. But before doing so, a few background words on the development of doctrine are needed.

Only in the nineteenth century did theologians begin to formulate explicit theories to explain how the development of doctrine occurred. An organic model developed from the views of Johann Möhler of the Catholic faculty at Tübingen and John Cardinal Newman. They viewed revelation as an idea grasped as an indistinct whole. Doctrines that attempted to express it grew like an organism, developing new expressions while remaining essentially the same. Variations on this view have been proposed by a number of main-line Catholic theologians.[35] Karl Rahner argued that recognition of the historical and cultural conditioning of doctrines necessarily leads to the conclusion that earlier formulations were approximations to the revealed truth that the doctrines were meant to express.[36] Most theologians agree that foundational revelation is closed with the apostles, but they recognize that revelation takes priority over dogmas. Revelation is graced experience. Words are always inadequate to express God's self-communication. The history of faith and the development of doctrine depends on God's grace, on divine initiative. New insights will of course be consistent with the totality of the faith as earlier understood, but new understandings, new truths, are possible.[37]

Based upon what we have described as our evolved human heritage, and upon the nature of revelation and its relationship to doctrine, it follows that doctrine must evolve with the human race. With revelation as interpersonal communion with God responded to with faith, and doctrine as the Church's attempt to articulate that experience, using the human mind and its cultural and historical inheritance, it is evident that doctrine is a divine-human product in which revealed truth is formulated in an imperfect and limited way. If the human side evolves, so will its formulations.

Usually doctrine does not change until circumstances force a change, until some crisis arises and the Church gathers to define something to guide the people of God in a new situation. New theological insights follow the clash with new problems. It might be fun to speculate about how our theology of evolution might help in a possible future event: the encounter with extra-terrestrial intelligence.

Since we are taking a long view, we realize that encounter with other intelligent life might take a hundred years, or thousands. Or it might happen next week. It is clear in the science community that the possibility of finding other life in the universe is considered increasingly probable. For many scientists, contact with intelligent life is judged to be just a matter of time, and every new step is tremendously exciting—the first stars with planets have been found in the last few years. Suppose, for purposes of our imaginative game, that they are right and contact is made.

Back when we were considering the clues about the divine nature and our own contained in the process of evolution, we noted that any theology consistent with evolution should take a long view of things, imagining our world and our species to go on for many thousands, perhaps millions of years. We said that it should be non-exclusive, related to the whole of creation of which we are but a tiny part. And we judged that it should be non-anthropocentric, not considering humanity as the only important part of God's creation, but recognizing how we are intimately related to the whole world ecology. With our modern understanding of Scripture as historically and culturally conditioned, we realize that God's covenant with the human race, described in Genesis, does not negate the possibility of other covenants with other of God's creatures in times and lands beyond our knowledge and ability even to imagine.

Our neoclassical theology proposes that the newly discovered beings are also God's creatures, called into existence to achieve the values of goodness and love, and to share their accomplishments with divinity itself. They are creatures made of the same elements as we are, obeying the same laws of nature, and so related to us just as we are related to the other creatures on our planet. Since they evolved as we did, called into creating themselves as we were, finite and self-seeking as we are, in all likelihood they too enter life in a state of original sin, and are in need of salvation. They needed no first parent, no Adam, of their race to be responsible for their plight. Their physical, biological and cultural evolution practically insures it. What we can be very sure of is that God loves them and wills their salvation. It is the divine nature to love.

Based on our theological model, we can also be sure that they have been recipients of divine revelation. They will have experienced the divine call from the first moments of their existence, and will have responded to it in varying degrees. Just how successful God has been in this self-revelation will depend upon how fully their race has responded. And this in turn depends upon their biological and cultural formation, the raw material with which God had to work. Their religion, or religions, will reflect the revelatory history of their own particular encounter with God. The level of success in that encounter will affect how they treat us. It is clear how we should treat them.

Expanding the message of biblical revelation to include them means recognizing that they are our neighbors, strangers whom we are called to love as we love ourselves, and as we love God. They will probably be very alien indeed. If we thought it was difficult to see other humans as neighbors, imagine what it will take to extend that concept to intelligent creatures that neither look nor act like human beings, and that appear very frightening to us. Knowing our human history of exploration and conquest, it is likely that aliens will be demonized though human fears and anxiety.

Human fears may well be justified. We don't know in what stage of civilization we will find these strangers. They may be races older and wiser than we are, in which case we would be most fortunate. Then again, they may be powerful and morally ambivalent, or even morally corrupt. A little reflection on human history will remind us that when more advanced peoples explored the new world, they did not shower good things upon its inhabitants. The native tribes were declared to be savages, sub-human and without souls. This allowed them to be subjugated, enslaved and exploited for whatever could be found of value. They were also subjected to accidental hazards associated with encounters with foreigners. The Europeans arriving in Mexico brought with them the diseases of the Old World which destroyed most of the population in a few years. Are today's Christians ready for the challenge of other intelligent life?

Suppose that ultimately humanity reaches some stable relationship with these others, and that mutual knowledge and understanding begins to grow. Hopefully this will occur right from the start. We will find, no doubt, that they have some kind of religion, some self-understanding of their purpose and place in the cosmos, some concepts of the transcendent and immanent One. In this post-Vatican II era, when we are more conscious of the presence of divine revelation in the world's religions, will we be able to recognize that presence in alien religions? What does one look for? Wouldn't one look for the same definitive revelation we have received through Jesus Christ—namely, that God *is* love and has established a covenant with his creatures to save them from sin and death? This is the "good news" that grounds the "deposit of faith" for Christians. Maybe, in such an encounter, we will learn much about ourselves. It would seem that a theology that assists in an alien encounter should be just as helpful in enlightening ecumenical efforts and the encounter with the world's religions.

Consider some of the fascinating theological challenges an encounter with extra-terrestrial intelligence would bring. Is it possible that the second person of the Trinity has become incarnate on other worlds? A theology of evolution must be non-exclusive, and non-anthropocentric. Is the dignity and worth of the human race in any way reduced by this possibility? Didn't Jesus say, "In my Father's house there are many mansions" (Jn 14:2)?

What about the mission of the Church? Is the command to "Go and teach all nations" limited to the planet earth? Did Christ come only to save the human race? If we had the chance to spread God's word to an alien race, should we do so? Recall that the early Church struggled with the idea of confining the early Church to the Jews. It was Paul who convinced them to carry the message of Christ to the Gentiles. Suppose it is agreed that the Christian message should be spread off-world. Should aliens be brought into the Church? Can the body of Christ have tentacles or other alien features? Or will the diversity and value of revelation both in other religions on earth and elsewhere be more clearly recognized? Perhaps our view of God's creation and covenant is too small. It would be helpful if we could develop a theology capable of dealing with what the future is likely to hold. It is possible that by developing a theology of evolution, we may come to better understand the divine-human relationship more deeply, even if other intelligent life in the universe is never found.

We close these speculations, and our reflections in this book on the areas of revelation science, and original sin, with this observation. Catholic theology has a long history of using the best of human knowledge in support of the faith. We should continue to do so. Notre Dame philosopher of science Ernan McMullin has made the following suggestion: "When an apparent conflict arises between a strongly supported scientific theory and some item of Christian doctrine, the Christian ought to look very carefully to the credentials of the doctrine. It may well be when he does so, the scientific understanding will enable the doctrine to be reformulated in a more adequate way."[38] May the Spirit lead us into a future where this will be done.

Notes

Preface

1. *The New York Times*, October 27, 1996.
2. Pastoral Constitution on the Church in the Modern World, 62.
3. *Theological Investigations*, XXI (New York: Crossroad, 1988), 104–05.
4. St. Augustine, *The Literal Meaning of Genesis*, I. 19. 39, trans. John Taylor, S.J., 2 vols. (New York: Newman Press, 1982), 42–43.
5. The interaction of science and religion is on the rise today, as is evidenced by the presentation of science-related papers at meetings of the Catholic Theological Society of America, by the activities and journals of groups such as The Center for Theology and the Natural Sciences, and *Zygon: Journal of Religion and Science*, and by the regular appearance of scientifically cognizant articles in journals such as *Horizons*. See, for example, Anne M. Clifford's "Postmodern Scientific Cosmology and the Christian God of Creation," *Horizons* 21, no. 1 (Spring 1994): 62–84.

Introduction

1. See *The New York Times*, October 27, 1996, concerning the Pope's address to the Pontifical Academy of Sciences. The Vatican, through the offices of the Vatican Observatory, sponsored a conference on Biological Evolution and Divine Action in the Universe at Castel Gondolfo during the summer of 1996. For earlier specula-

tions of Pope John Paul II on evolution, see "Message of Pope John Paul II to the Reverend George V. Coyne, S.J., Director of the Vatican Observatory," *Physics, Philosophy and Theology: A Common Quest for Understanding*, ed. Robert J. Russell, William R. Stoeger, S.J., and George V. Coyne, S.J. (Vatican Observatory: Libreria Editrice Vaticana, 1988), M12.

2. *Catechism of the Catholic Church* (Mahwah, N.J.: Paulist Press, 1994).

3. Joseph Cardinal Ratzinger and Christoph Schönborn, *Introduction to the Catechism of the Catholic Church* (San Francisco: Ignatius Press, 1994), 71.

4. *Catechism of the Catholic Church*, paragraph 400.

5. Bishop (now Cardinal) Schönborn, in *Introduction to the Catechism of the Catholic Church*, 62, obviously sensitive to criticisms received on this subject, claims that evolution is discussed several times (he notes paragraphs 283, 284, 285, 302, and 310). A check of these paragraphs reveals no mention of the subject.

6. "Creation and Original Sin" in *Commentary on the Catechism of the Catholic Church*, ed. Michael J. Walsh (Collegeville, Minn,: Liturgical Press, 1994), 94. The numbers in parenthesis are the paragraph numbers in *Catechism*.

7. *The New York Times*, July 26, 1992, E5.

1. The Church and Evolution—A Brief History

1. See Thomas A. Goudge, "Evolutionism," *Dictionary of the History of Ideas*, ed. Phillip P. Wiener (New York: Charles Scribner's Sons, 1973).

2. *Timaeus* 29e.

3. *Timaeus* 30c, d.

4. For the fascinating history of this and related ideas, see Arthur O. Lovejoy, *The Great Chain of Being: A Study of the History of an Idea* (Cambridge, Mass.: Harvard University Press, 1936).

5. *Metaphysics*, III, 1003a. See Lovejoy, 58 for a discussion of Aristotle's various criteria of ranking.

6. Lovejoy, *The Great Chain of Being*, 59.

7. "The City of God," in *Basic Writings of Saint Augustine*, vol.

2, ed. Whitney J. Oates, trans. M. Dods, G. Wilson, and J. J. Smith (Grand Rapids, Mich.: Baker Book House, 1948), 208.

8. See his *The Literal Meaning of Genesis*, vol. 1, 1–6.

9. There have been some Catholic writers who have used this idea of Augustine's to enlist his support for evolution, but it is recognized today that this is going beyond the facts. As philosopher of science Ernan McMullin says, "Augustine did not hold that one species could arise out of another; his theory of forms as ideas in the mind of God would have rendered such an hypothesis quite implausible" (*Evolution and Creation*, ed. Ernan McMullin (Notre Dame, Ind.: University of Notre Dame Press, 1985), 15.

10. See his *Summa Contra Gentiles*, II, 45, for a variety of these arguments.

11. *Summa Contra Gentiles*, I, 80, 4.

12. Goudge, "Evolutionism," 176.

13. McMullin, *Evolution and Creation*, 16.

14. In the more orthodox version, the chain extends only to the highest kind of creature, between which and the Absolute Being there is assumed to be an infinite gap. See especially Lovejoy, 59. See also Ernan McMullin, "Introduction: Evolution and Creation," in *Evolution and Creation*.

15. Lovejoy, 242.

16. See Goudge's article for plentiful details on the history of this period.

17. This section relies principally on two sources. First, Zoltán Alszeghy, S.J., "Development in the Doctrinal Formulation of the Church concerning the Theory of Evolution," *The Evolving World and Theology*, ed. Johannes Metz, vol. 26 of *Concilium* (New York: Paulist Press, 1967), and second, Ervin Nemesszeghy, S.J. and John Russell, S.J., *Theology of Evolution* (Butler, Wis.: Clergy Book Service, 1971).

18. From the *Dogmatic Constitution on the Catholic Faith*, 4. See Nemesszeghy, 40.

19. Alszeghy, 27.

20. Ibid., 28.

21. Ibid., 29.

22. The translations are taken from Nemesszeghy and Russell, 47 and 61.

23. A quotation attributed to theologian Henri de Lubac; see Leo J. O'Donovan, S.J., "Was Vatican II Evolutionary? A Note on Conciliar Language," *Theological Studies* 36 (1975): 495.

24. Translation from Austin Flannery, O.P., ed., *Vatican Council II: The Conciliar and Post Conciliar Documents* (Newport, New York: Costello Publishing Company, 1975).

25. See the conclusions of the volume by Nemesszeghy and Russell, for example, and Zachary Hayes, O.F.M., *What Are They Saying About Creation?* (New York: Paulist Press, 1980), 53.

26. "Message to the Director of the Vatican Observatory," in *Physics, Philosophy and Theology: A Quest for Common Understanding,* ed. Robert J. Russell, William R. Stoeger, S.J., and George V. Coyne, S.J. (Vatican City State: Libreria Editrice Vaticana, 1988), M13.

27. Ibid., M11.

28. *The New York Times,* Sunday, October 27, 1996.

29. See the quotation from *Humani Generis* earlier in this chapter, and note 21.

2. Origins of Original Sin

1. Henri Rondet, S.J., *Original Sin: The Patristic and Theological Background,* trans. Cajetan Finegan, O.P. (Staten Island, N.Y.: Alba House, 1972), 122.

2. Several good sources are: Walter Brueggemann, *Genesis* (Atlanta: John Knox Press, 1982), 41; John J. Scullion, *Genesis: A Commentary for Students, Teachers, and Preachers* (Collegeville, Minn.: The Liturgical Press, 1992), 42; Bruce Vawter, *On Genesis* (Garden City, N.Y.: Doubleday, 1977), 90; and Claus Westermann, *Creation,* trans. John J. Scullion, S.J. (Philadelphia: Fortress Press, 1974), 89. See also Herbert Haag, *Is Original Sin in Scripture?* trans. Dorothy Thompson (New York: Sheed and Ward, 1969).

3. *Original Sin,* 21.

4. Paul's exegesis may have been influenced by late Jewish theological speculations, such as 4 Esdras in the Appendix to the Latin Vulgate (2 Esdras in the NRSV). "O Adam, what have you done? For

though it was you who sinned, the fall was not yours alone, but ours also who are your descendants" (2 Esdras 7.48/118). See also Brueggemann, *Genesis*, 42.

5. See, for example, Joseph A. Fitzmyer, S.J., "The Letter to the Romans," in *The New Jerome Biblical Commentary*, ed. Raymond E. Brown, S.S., Joseph A. Fitzmyer, S.J., and Roland E. Murphy, O. Carm. (Englewood Cliffs, N.J.: Prentice Hall, 1990), 845.

6. *I Clement*, ch. 12. *Ante-Nicene Fathers*, vol. 9, ed. Allan Menzies (1896; Peabody Mass.: Hendrickson Publishers, Inc., 1994), 232. Hereafter referred to as ANF followed by the volume and page numbers—e.g., ANF 9.232.

7. *Epistle of Ignatius to the Trallians*, ch. 8, ANF 1.69.

8. *Epistle of Barnabas*, ch. 5, ANF 1.139.

9. *Justin's Dialogue with Trypho*, ch. 100, ANF 1.249.

10. *Address of Tatian to the Greeks*, ch. 7, ANF 2.68.

11. *Original Sin*, 31. Angels, demons, and the supernatural order were a major preoccupation of Christian theologians during the first three centuries. See Jaroslav Pelikan, *The Emergence of the Catholic Tradition (100–600)* (Chicago: The University of Chicago Press, 1971), 132–141, 148.

12. *Theophilus to Autolycus*, ch. 29, ANF 2.105.

13. *Original Sin*, 38.

14. Irenaeus, *Against Heresies*, IV, ch. 38, 3, ANF 1.521–22.

15. Ibid., III, ch. 21, 10, ANF 1.454.

16. *A Treatise on the Soul*, ch. 6, ANF 3.186.

17. Ibid., ch. 40, ANF 3.220.

18. *Original Sin*, 61.

19. *On Baptism*, ch. 18, ANF 3.678.

20. *The Epistle to the Romans*, ch. 5. Translation from *Original Sin*, 80.

21. *Original Sin*, 74–84.

22. *Original Sin*, 64–65.

23. *On the Making of Man*, ch. 16, 16. *Nicene and Post-Nicene Fathers*, Second Series, vol. 5, ed. Philip Schaff, and Henry Wace (Peabody, Mass.: Hendrickson Publishers, Inc., 1995), 406. There are two series each of 14 volumes to be referred to as NPNF[1] and NPNF[2].

24. Ibid., ch. 17, 2 and ch. 18, 9.

25. *Oration* 38, 4, NPNF[2] 7.345–6.

26. *The Epistle to the Romans*, Homily 10, 19, NPNF[1] 11.403.

27. John Meyendorff, *Byzantine Theology: Historical Trends and Doctrinal Themes* (New York: Fordham University Press, 1974), 145.

28. *On the Decease of His Brother Satyrus*, Book 2, 6, NPNF[2] 10.175.

29. *On the Mysteries*, ch. 6, NPNF[2] 10.321.

30. See Rondet's *Original Sin*, 112, and J. N. D. Kelly's *Early Christian Doctrines* (San Francisco: HarperCollins Publishers, 1978), 353–55.

31. Pelikan argues that these factors were premises from which conclusions could be drawn about the fall and original sin: *The Emergence of the Catholic Tradition (100–600)*, 286.

32. Good overviews of this period can be found in Jaroslav Pelikan, *The Emergence of the Catholic Tradition (100–600)*, 141–71 and 278–318; J. N. D. Kelly, *Early Christian Doctrines*, 163–88 and 344–74; Henri Rondet S.J., *Original Sin*.

33. See *The Confessions of St. Augustine*, trans. John K. Ryan (Garden City, N.Y.: Doubleday and Company, 1960).

34. The definitive biography of Augustine in our day is that of Peter Brown, *Augustine of Hippo* (Berkeley and Los Angeles: University of California Press, 1967).

35. Brown, 42.

36. *The City of God*, 204.

37. Ibid., 610, 233 and 582.

38. Ibid., 273. See John H. Wright, "Predestination," in *The New Dictionary of Theology*, ed. Joseph A. Komonchak, Mary Collins, and Dermot A. Lane (Collegeville, Minn.: The Liturgical Press, 1987), 797.

39. Augustine presents his detailed interpretation of the first three chapters of *Genesis* in *The Literal Interpretation of Genesis;* see especially Vol. 2. The broad story is summarized in *The City of God*, Books XIII and XIV.

40. *The City of God*, 221.

41. Ibid., 220.

42. *Against Julian*, trans. A. Schumacher (New York: Fathers of the Church, Inc., 1957), 158.

43. Augustine's views on sex were widely influential during the patristic period. Later, Aquinas said that the marriage act was meritorious if performed for procreation or as a matter of justice, to render the marriage debt, but if the motive was sexual pleasure it was sinful (*Summa Theologica,* Supplement, Q. 41, 4. Hereafter referred to as *ST*). Pope Innocent XI in 1679 condemned the idea that the marriage act performed for pleasure alone was free from sin *(The Christian Faith in the Doctrinal Documents of the Catholic Church,* ed. J. Neuner, S.J. and J. Dupuis, S.J. (New York: Alba House, 1982), 662.

44. *The City of God,* 214, 220.

45. *Opus Imperfectum Contra Julianum,* 6, 27. See Elaine Pagels, *Adam, Eve, and the Serpent* (New York: Vintage Books, 1988), Chapter VI, especially 134.

46. For example, see *The City of God,* 644ff.

47. The early Fathers, and especially Augustine, were convinced that the Roman gods were in fact fallen angels, which accounted for their lustful decadent lives. According to Augustine, the Roman worship of these evil spirits was responsible for the fall of the Roman empire; see the first ten books of *The City of God.*

48. *Against Julian,* 115.

49. Ibid., 218.

50. *The Literal Meaning of Genesis,* vol. 2, 110.

51. "The Sixteenth Council of Carthage" (418), in *The Christian Faith in the Doctrinal Documents of the Catholic Church,* 135, 138.

52. Translation from J. Patout Burns, S.J., *Theological Anthropology* (Philadelphia: Fortress Press, 1981), 113.

53. *Cur Deus Homo* (Why God Became Man), in *St. Anselm: Basic Writings,* trans. S. N. Deane (LaSalle, Ill.: Open Court, 1979).

54. "The Virginal Conception and Original Sin (Selections)," in *A Scholastic Miscellany: Anselm to Ockham,* ed. and trans. Eugene R. Fairweather (Philadelphia: The Westminster Press, 1956), 184–200.

55. Ibid., 197–98.

56. See *ST*, Ia. QQ. 95–101; Ia–IIae. QQ. 81–83.

57. *ST*, IIIa, Q. 69, ad 3.

58. "Bondage of the Will," *Martin Luther: Selections from His Writings*, ed. John Dillenberger (Garden City, New York: Doubleday and Company, 1961), 203.

59. "Lectures on Romans," ch. 12, *The Library of Christian Classics,* vol. 15, ed. and trans. Wilhelm Pauck (Philadelphia: The Westminster Press, 1961), 167.

60. *Against Two Letters of the Pelagians*, I, 7; NPNF[1] 5.379, written sometime after 420. Augustine wrote *On Free Choice of the Will* between 388 and 391, around the time of his baptism. Augustine's success in maintaining both the necessity of God's grace and free will has been the subject of much scholarly discussion. Most scholars judge that he maintained the necessity for both throughout his life. See Eugene Portalié, S.J., *A Guide to the Thought of Saint Augustine,* trans R. H. Bastian (Chicago: Henry Regnery Company, 1960), and Etienne Gilson, *The Christian Philosophy of Saint Augustine* (New York: Random House, 1960). Preventing complete confidence in this view is the enigmatic statement in his *Retractions,* II, 1, "I have tried hard to maintain the free choice of the human will, but the grace of God prevailed."

61. *Commentaries on the Epistle of Paul the Apostle to the Romans*, ch. 5:12, trans. and ed. Rev. John Owen (Grand Rapids, Mich.: Baker Book House, 1996), 200–201.

62. *Institutes of the Christian Religion*, ed. John T. McNeill, trans. Ford Lewis Battles (Philadelphia: The Westminister Press, 1960) vol. 2, book IV, ch. 15, 20.

63. "Decree on Original Sin," The General Council of Trent, in *The Christian Faith in the Doctrinal Documents of the Catholic Church*, 137–39.

3. Post-Vatican II Advances

1. "Vatican II's Constitution on Revelation: History and Interpretation," *Theological Studies* 28 (1967): 51–75.

2. Ibid., 57.

3. *Retrieving Fundamental Theology: The Three Styles of Contemporary Theology* (New York: Paulist Press, 1993), 1.

4. Ibid., 49.

5. Ibid., 131–32.

6. Jerry D. Korsmeyer, *God–Creature–Revelation: A Neoclassical Framework for Fundamental Theology* (Lanham, Md.: University Press of America, 1995), 161–65.

7. O'Collins, 76–78. He references *Gaudium et spes*, 4, 11 and 44, as well as other documents.

8. *Dei verbum*, 12. I have quoted the Abbott translation on the advice of O'Collins, 139. *The Documents of Vatican II*, ed. Walter M. Abbott, S.J. and Joseph Gallagher (New York: The America Press, 1966), 120.

9. See ch. 2, n. 2. And add, as other sources relied upon by Catholic scholars: *Creation in the Old Testament*, ed. Bernard W. Anderson (Philadelphia: Fortress Press, 1984); Gerhard Von Rad, *Genesis* (Philadelphia: The Westminster Press, 1972); and E. A. Speiser, *Genesis* (Garden City, N.Y.: Doubleday and Company, 1981).

10. Pope John Paul II, in an address to the Pontifical Academy of Science in October, 1981, particularly reiterated this point.

> The Bible itself speaks to us of the origin of the universe and its makeup, not in order to provide us with a scientific treatise but in order to state the correct relationships of man with God and with the universe. Sacred Scripture wishes simply to declare that the world was created by God, and in order to reach this truth it expresses itself in the terms of the cosmology in use at the time of the writer. The Sacred Book likewise wishes to tell men that the world was not created as the seat of the gods, as was taught by other cosmogonies and cosmologies, but was rather created for the service of man and the glory of God. Any other teaching about the origin and make-up of the universe is alien to the intentions of the Bible, which does not wish to teach how the heavens were made but how one goes to heaven.

In Francisco J. Ayala, "The Theory of Evolution: Recent Successes and Challenges," *Evolution and Creation*, ed. Ernan McMullin (Notre Dame, Ind.: University of Notre Dame Press, 1985), 61.

11. *Genesis*, 41.

12. See Rosemary Radford Ruether, *Sexism and God-Talk:*

Toward a Feminist Theology (Boston: Beacon Press, 1983), 37, and Anne M. Clifford, "When Being Human Becomes Truly Earthly: An Ecofeminist Proposal for Solidarity," in *In the Embrace of God: Feminist Approaches to Theological Anthropology*, ed. Ann O'Hara Graff (Maryknoll, N.Y.: Orbis Books, 1995), 173–89.

13. *On Genesis*, 90.

14. Pontifical Biblical Commission, "The Interpretation of the Bible in the Church," *Origins* 23, no. 29 (January 6, 1994).

15. Ibid., 524.

16. Ibid., 510.

17. Scholarship on original sin from just before Vatican II until recently has been very well summarized in three articles in *Theological Studies* appearing at roughly ten year intervals: James L. Conner, S.J., "Original Sin: Contemporary Approaches," *Theological Studies* 29 (1968): 215–40; Brian O. McDermott, S. J., "Original Sin: Recent Developments," *Theological Studies* 38 (1977): 478–512; Stephen J. Duffy, "Our Hearts of Darkness: Original Sin Revisited," *Theological Studies* 49 (1988): 597–622.

18. See Conner, 219–22, and Duffy, 599.

19. McDermott, 484, and Duffy, 618–19.

20. In *Commentary on the Catechism of the Catholic Church*, 98.

21. Francis A. Sullivan, *S.J., Creative Fidelity: Weighing and Interpreting Documents of the Magisterium* (New York: Paulist Press, 1996), 40. In a recent review of this book, Ladislas Orsy, S.J., another expert in doctrinal interpretation, notes, "S.'s book, clear and competent, should be compulsory reading in every school of theology...." (*Theological Studies* 58, no. 1 [March 1997]): 178.

22. Ibid., 7.

23. Daly, in *The New Dictionary of Theology*, 728, and Conner, 222–25.

24. As Henri Rondet, S.J., noted in his *Original Sin*, concerning the Council of Trent: "The question of the historicity or non-historicity of the account of the fall did not even cross the minds of the conciliar fathers." They believed as people of their times (273).

25. See Duffy, 615.

26. Ibid., 617.

27. *The Phenomenon of Man.*, trans. Bernard Wall (1955; New York: Harper & Brothers, 1959), 218.

28. Pierre Teilhard de Chardin, *Christianity and Evolution*, trans. René Hague (New York: Harcourt Brace Jovanovich, Inc., 1969), 183.

29. *The Phenomenon of Man*, 297–98.

30. In essays written in the early 1980s, the very orthodox Karl Rahner chided the Church for its treatment of Teilhard and its failure to pick up and develop his insights, *Theological Investigations*, vol. XXI, trans. Hugh M. Riley (New York: Crossroad, 1988), 25, 227. His influence also continues outside Catholicism; see a recent issue of a journal of religion and science devoted to his work, *Zygon* 30, no. 1 (March 1995).

31. See several essays in his *Christianity and Evolution* 45 and 187. See McDermott, 496–98, for a review of Karl Schmitz-Moormann's work on original sin, an extension of Teilhard's comments on the subject.

32. Ibid. 194–95.

33. In *Christianity and Evolution*, 233, n. 7, Teilhard says, "It is embarrassing (unless it was meant as a joke) to read in *Time* (15 September 1952) the advice given by a teacher of theology (Fr. Francis J. Connell, Dean of Theology) to be wary of pilots of 'flying saucers': if they landed from a planet not affected by original sin, they would be *unkillable*."

34. Conner, 227.

35. *God's World in the Making* (Pittsburgh, Pa.: Duquesne University Press, 1964), 33.

36. Ibid., 83. See Conner, 229–31, for his review of Schoonenberg's work.

37. *God in Creation and Evolution*. trans. Martin Versfeld (New York: Sheed and Ward, 1965), 27. See also Conner, 231–34.

38. Ibid., 47.

39. Ibid., 28. The sexist language mars the presentation.

40. *Hominisation: The Evolutionary Origin of Man as a Theological Problem.*, trans. W. J. O'Hara (1958; New York: Herder and Herder, 1965).

41. See Karl Rahner, "Evolution and Original Sin," trans. Theodore L. Westow, in *The Evolving World and Theology*, ed. Johannes Metz (New York: Paulist Press, 1967), 67.

42. McDermott, 478–504.

43. George Vandervelde, *Original Sin: Two Contemporary Roman Catholic Approaches* (Washington, D.C.: University Press of America, 1981).

44. Rahner has a long string of articles that touch on various aspects of original sin. A good summary of his position is presented in "Original Sin," in *Encyclopedia of Theology: The Concise Sacramentum Mundi*, ed. Karl Rahner (New York: Crossroad, 1982), 1148–55. See also "The Sin of Adam," *Theological Investigations* XI, 247–62, and *Foundations of Christian Faith: An Introduction to the Idea of Christianity*, trans. William V. Dyck (New York: Crossroad, 1984), 106–15. McDermott in his review article discusses the very similar position of Weger, 478–82.

45. *Vorfragen zu einem ökumenischen Amtsverständnis* (Freiburg: Herder, 1974), 37. See also McDermott's review article, 484–85.

46. Conner, 229.

47. See McDermott, 493–96.

48. Ibid., 495.

49. Ibid., 495–96.

50. Ibid., 498–502.

51. *Original Sin: Two Major Trends in Contemporary Roman Catholic Reinterpretation*. See also McDermott's comments on this, 505–8.

52. Ibid., 313–18.

53. Ibid., 283–86.

54. Ibid., 326–34, McDermott, 508.

55. McDermott, 512.

56. "Our Hearts of Darkness," *Theological Studies* 49.

57. Ibid., 621.

58. Ibid., 610.

59. Ibid., 612.

60. S. Moore, "Original Sin, Resurrection, and Trinity," *Lonergan Workshop* 4 (1983) 85–98.

61. Duffy, 615.

62. Ibid., 617–18.

63. Ibid., 620.

64. Ibid.

65. For this insight see Paul Achtemeier, *Romans* (Atlanta: John Knox Press, 1985), 95.

4. Evolution: Problem or Clue?

1. See the "Typical American" poll results in *The New York Times*, Sunday, July 26, 1992.

2. *Summa Contra Gentiles* II. 3.

3. For an explanation of the different relationships that can exist between science and religion see John F. Haught, *Science and Religion: From Conflict to Conversation* (New York: Paulist Press, 1995).

4. Some of the best writers of popular science fall into this category: Carl Sagan, Stephen Jay Gould, Edward O. Wilson, Steven Weinberg, and Stephen W. Hawking come to mind.

5. Stephen Hawking's claim that his theory of cosmic origins negates the need for a Creator God has become notorious as an example of this kind of misunderstanding. See *A Brief History of Time: From the Big Bang to Black Holes* (New York: Bantam Books, 1988), 144.

6. See Ronald L. Numbers, *The Creationists: The Evolution of Scientific Creationism* (Berkeley and Los Angeles: University of California Press, 1992).

7. Carl Sagan did finally recognize that what he called "liberal" religion was not his enemy. "Of course many religions—devoted to reverence, awe, ethics, ritual, community, family, charity, and political and economic justice—are in no way challenged, but rather uplifted, by the findings of science. There is no necessary conflict between science and religion. On one level, they share similar and consonant roles, and each needs the other" *(The Demon-Haunted World: Science as a Candle in the Dark* [New York: Random House, 1995], 277).

8. American Museum of Natural History poll reported in *The New York Times*, April 21, 1994.

9. There are many popular accounts of the evolution of the cosmos and of biological life. We will refer to a number of them as we proceed. Three are recommended that provide good overviews of different parts of the story. First, for a general overview of the development of knowledge of the cosmos and its evolution, Timothy Ferris, *Coming of Age in the Milky Way* (New York: William Morrow and Company, 1988). Next, for an overview of biological evolution, Maitland A. Edey and Donald C. Johanson, *Blueprints: Solving the Mystery of Evolution* (Boston: Little, Brown and Company, 1989); and then for human evolution, Steve Jones, Robert Martin and David Pilbeam, eds., *The Cambridge Encyclopedia of Human Evolution* (Cambridge: Cambridge University Press, 1992).

10. Scientists and theologians are left free to speculate whether or not there were cosmic epochs before our own, perhaps a series of big bangs and big crunches as universes expanded, and then contracted to start the process all over again. Scientifically there is no way for cosmologists to gain any information before this singularity, since, according to the theory, even the laws of nature were not in existence at the moment of the big bang. For some speculation on these matters by scientists and theologians see Robert John Russell, Nancey Murphy and C. J. Isham, eds., *Quantum Cosmology and the Laws of Nature: Scientific Perspectives on Divine Action* (Vatican City State: Vatican Observatory Publications, 1993). For more exotic theories, see Timothy Ferris, *The Whole Shebang: A State-of-the-Universe(s) Report* (New York: Simon & Schuster), 1997.

11. For a splendid two-page summary of the cosmic story see John Polkinghorne, *The Faith of a Physicist: Reflections of a Bottom-Up Thinker* (Princeton: Princeton University Press, 1994), 71–72.

12. See *Coming of Age in the Milky Way*, 278, for a chart of the abundance of elements in the universe, and information about the scientists who have worked out the details of element formation.

13. Estimates taken from Carl Sagan and Ann Druyan, *Shadows of Forgotten Ancestors: A Search for Who We Are* (New York: Random House, 1992), 13.

14. Claude J. Allègre and Stephen H. Schneider, "The Evolution of the Earth," *Scientific American: Special Issue, Life in the Universe* (October 1994): 66–75.

15. See *Blueprints*, especially chapters 15–17, and Leslie E. Orgel, "The Origin of Life on Earth," *Scientific American* (October 1994): 77–83.

16. See Stuart Kauffman, *At Home in the Universe: The Search of the Laws of Self-Organization and Complexity* (New York: Oxford University Press, 1995).

17. See Edward O. Wilson, *The Diversity of Life* (Cambridge, Mass.: The Belnap Press of the Harvard University Press, 1992).

18. Don Lessem, *Dinosaurs Rediscovered: New Findings Which Are Revolutionizing Dinosaur Science* (New York: Touchstone, 1992), 35. See also David B. Weishampel, Peter Dodson, and Halszka Osmólska, eds., *The Dinosauria* (Berkeley: University of California Press, 1990).

19. Tom Gehrels, "Collisions with Comets and Asteroids," *Scientific American* (March 1996): 54–59.

20. *The Cambridge Encyclopedia*, 199.

21. Ibid., 231–40.

22. See Ian Tattersall, *The Fossil Trail: How We Know What We Think We Know About Human Evolution* (New York: Oxford University Press, 1995), 229–35. In addition to *The Cambridge Encyclopedia of Human Evolution* and *Blueprints*, see Richard Leakey and Roger Lewin, *Origins Reconsidered: In Search of What Makes Us Human* (New York: Doubleday, 1992), and Donald Johanson and James Shreeve, *Lucy's Child: The Discovery of a Human Ancestor* (New York: William Morrow, 1989).

23. See *The Cambridge Encyclopedia*, 294, and *Shadows of Forgotten Ancestors*, 277.

24. David Pilbeam, "What Makes Us Human?" *The Cambridge Encyclopedia*, 5.

25. *Shadows of Forgotten Ancestors*, 314–15.

26. *The Fossil Trail*, 247.

27. See, for example, Frank White, *The Overview Effect: Space Exploration and Human Evolution* (Boston: Houghton Mifflin Company, 1987).

28. "In the United States a quarter of all prescriptions dispensed by pharmacies are substances extracted from plants. Another 13 percent come from microorganisms and 3 percent more from animals,

for a total of over 40 percent that are organism-derived" (*The Diversity of Life*, 283–85; for numbers of species, see 132–62).

29. See *The Diversity of Life*: "So important are insects and other land-dwelling arthropods that if all were to disappear, humanity probably could not last more than a few months" (133).

30. Ibid., 278–80.

31. Carl Sagan, "The Search for Extraterrestrial Life," *Scientific American* (October 1994): 92–99.

32. Christian de Duve, *Vital Dust: Life as a Cosmic Imperative* (New York: HarperCollins, 1995), 292.

33. Co-creators is a term put forth by Lutheran theologian Philip Hefner to describe his Theology of the Created Co-Creator; see *The Human Factor: Evolution, Culture and Religion* (Minn.: Fortress Press, 1993).

34. *Christianity and Evolution*, 231–32.

35. Walter J. Ong, S.J., "Do We Live in a Post-Christian Age?" *America* (February 3, 1996): 18.

36. *New York Times* National Edition (October 1, 1995).

37. In a recent article, Peter Phan has suggested that process theology could enrich our views of eschatology by adding insights concerning the "relational and evolving natue of all reality." See his "Contemporary Contexts and Issues in Eschatology," *Theological Studies* 55, no. 3 (September 1994): 335–36.

38. Stephen Jay Gould, *Wonderful Life: The Burgess Shale and the Nature of History* (New York: W. W. Norton & Company, 1989), 51.

5. Toward a Theology of Evolution

1. For a history and explanation of this and other philosophical concepts of God see Charles Hartshorne and William L. Reese, *Philosophers Speak of God* (Chicago: The University of Chicago Press, 1953).

2. Whitehead's main work defining his metaphysics is *Process and Reality, Corrected Edition*, ed. D. R. Griffin and D. W. Sherburne (1929; New York: The Free Press, 1978). Hartshorne's concept of divinity is best presented in *The Divine Relativity; A*

Social Conception of God (New Haven: Yale University Press, 1948). See also Hartshorne's *The Logic of Perfection and Other Essays in Neoclassical Metaphysics* (LaSalle, Ill.: Open Court, 1962), and *Creative Synthesis and Philosophic Method* (1970; Lanham, Md.: University Press of America, 1983).

3. Hartshorne calls this characteristic of divinity "dual transcendence." See his *Creative Synthesis and Philosophic Method*, 243, and *The Logic of Perfection*, 42–43.

4. Some Catholic theologians using process thought include Joseph A. Bracken, S.J., who has several fine volumes: *The Triune Symbol: Persons, Process and Community* (Lanham, Md.: University Press of America, 1985); *Society and Spirit: A Trinitarian Cosmology* (Selinsgrove: Susquehanna University Press, 1991); and *The Divine Matrix: Creativity as Link between East and West* (Maryknoll, New York: Orbis Books, 1995). See also Barry L. Whitney, *Evil and the Process God* (New York: The Edwin Mellen Press, 1985), and *What Are They Saying About God And Evil?* (New York: Paulist Press, 1989). Others who have appropriated process thought into their work include David Tracy, *Blessed Rage for Order* (New York: Seabury, 1975), and John F. Haught, *The Cosmic Adventure: Science, Religion and the Quest for Purpose* (New York: Paulist Press, 1984), and his *Science and Religion*, noted in ch. 4.

5. A number of studies in recent years have pointed out the inadequacy of the classical concept of divine *agape*. See Daniel Day Williams, *The Spirit and the Forms of Love* (New York: Harper & Row, 1968), and Ceslaus Spicq, O.P., *Agape in the New Testament*, 3 vols., trans. Sister Marie Aquinas McNamara, O.P., and Sister Mary Honoria Richter, O.P. (St. Louis: B. Herder Book Co., 1963, 1965, 1966).

6. For a description of a consistent neoclassical model for Catholic fundamental theology see my *God–Creature–Revelation: A Neoclassical Framework for Fundamental Theology* (Lanham, Md.: University Press of America, 1995).

7. See Sallie McFague, "Models of God for an Ecological, Evolutionary Era: God as Mother of the Universe," in *Physics, Philosophy and Theology* (see Introduction, n. 1).

8. *The Phenomenon of Man*, 299–301.

9. *Summa Contra Gentiles* I, 84. 3.

10. For a process view of consciousness see David Ray Griffin, "What Is Consciousness and Why Is It So Problematic?" A talk given on February 13, 1992. Available from The Center for Process Studies, Claremont, CA.

11. This process of coming together Whitehead calls a "concrescence," which means becoming concrete, coming into actuality. See *Process and Reality*, 219ff.

12. Ibid., 219. Whitehead calls these feelings "prehensions."

13. See *God–Creature–Revelation*, 83ff., and chapter 4 for a process description of the divine-human interaction.

14. "What Is Consciousness?" 2. Consciousness is provoked into existence by a feeling of negation, Griffin tells us, "More precisely, consciousness is the awareness of the *contrast* between what is and what might be but isn't, between fact and theory" (28).

15. *Process and Reality*, 53, and 267.

16. John B. Cobb, Jr. and David Ray Griffin have done so in their *Process Theology: An Introductory Exposition* (Philadelphia: The Westminster Press, 1976), 87.

17. See Arthur C. Danto, "Persons," in *The Encyclopedia of Philosophy*, vol. 6 (New York: Macmillan Publishing Co., 1967), 110.

18. See John B. Cobb's *Matters of Life and Death* (Louisville, Kentucky: Westminster/John Knox Press, 1991).

19. Ibid., 35–38.

20. Marjorie Hewett Suchocki, *The End of Evil: Process Eschatology in Historical Context* (New York: The State University of New York Press, 1988). See especially Chapter VI.

21. These few remarks do not do justice to Suchocki's sophisticated and insightful vision of a possible human future. Further comment will have to await another time.

22. *Religion in an Age of Science* (New York: Harper & Row, 1990), 164.

23. See *God–Creature–Revelation*, 132–37, for more on evolution in the neoclassical model.

24. *Omnipotence and Other Theological Mistakes* (Albany: The State University of New York Press, 1984), 71.

25. See Charles L. Birch, "Chance, Purpose, and Darwinism," in *The Philosophy of Charles Hartshorne*, ed. Lewis E. Hahn (La Salle, Ill.: Open Court, 1991), 57–60; and Jerry D. Korsmeyer, *God–Creature–Revelation*, 137–40.

26. The idea of the "fall upward" with the evolution of consciousness is from Charles L. Birch and John B. Cobb, Jr., *The Liberation of Life* (Denton, Tex.: Environmental Ethics Books, 1990), 117–22. We will discuss this further in the next chapter when considering original sin.

27. "The Earth: A New Context for Religious Unity," in *Thomas Berry and the New Cosmology*, ed. Anne Lonergan and Caroline Richards (Mystic, Conn.: Twenty-Third Publications, 1987), 37.

28. *God–Creature–Revelation*, 174.

29. Ibid., ch. 6.

6. *Orignal Sin and the Future of Catholic Doctrine*

1. *The Symbolism of Evil*, trans. Emerson Buchanan (Boston: Beacon Press, 1967), 239.

2. "Sin," in *A Handbook of Christian Theology*, ed. Marvin Halverson and Arthur A. Cohen (New York: World Publishing, 1958), 349.

3. *The Symbolism of Evil*, 351.

4. Ibid., 348.

5. See Carl Sagan, *The Dragons of Eden: Speculations on the Evolution of Human Intelligence* (New York: Random House, 1977), 51–80.

6. See Paul D. MacLean, *A Triune Concept of the Brain and Behavior* (Toronto: University of Toronto Press, 1973). For the most recent formulation of his model see, "Women: A More Balanced Brain?" *Zygon* 31, No. 3 (September 1996): 421–39.

7. MacLean, *Zygon*: 426.

8. Ibid., 428.

9. Sagan, *The Dragons of Eden*, 69–71.

10. See Carl G. Jung, *The Undiscovered Self*, trans. R. F. C. Hull (Boston: Little, Brown and Company, 1957). For insight into how behavior evolves see Jean Piaget, *Behavior and Evolution*, trans.

Donald Nicholson-Smith (London: Routledge & Kegan Paul, 1979).

11. See Edward O. Wilson, *Sociobiology: The New Synthesis* (Cambridge, Mass.: The Belknap Press of Harvard University Press, 1975), and his *On Human Nature* (London: Harvard University Press, 1978). Wilson's own view is that of a materialist, and reductionist, which will bias religious people against some of his otherwise reasonable arguments. However, his presuppositions lead him to conclude that religions exist only because they are enabling mechanisms for group survival *(On Human Nature,* 3).

12. Adam Kuper, *The Chosen Primate: Human Nature and Cultural Diversity* (Cambridge, Mass.: Harvard University Press, 1994)

13. Ibid., 5–6.

14. Robert Ardrey, *African Genesis: A Personal Investigation into the Animal Origins and the Nature of Man* (London: Collins, 1961), and A. Alland, *The Human Imperative* (New York: Columbia University Press, 1972); also R. E. Leakey and R. Lewin, *Origins: What New Discoveries Reveal About the Emergence of Our Species and Its Possible Future* (London: Macdonald & Jane's, 1977).

15. *The Liberation of Life: From the Cell to the Community* (Denton, Tex.: Environmental Ethics Books, 1990), 110–22.

16. Ibid., 116.

17. Terrence W. Deacon, *The Cambridge Encyclopedia of Human Evolution*, 116–17.

18. Ibid., 117–23, and William H. Calvin, "The Emergence of Intelligence," *Scientific American* (October 1994): 100–07.

19. Tattersall, *The Fossil Trail*, 244.

20. Ibid., 245.

21. J. A. J. Gowlett, *The Cambridge Encyclopedia*, 345. For a discussion of the religious meaning of burial and of the art of early humanity see Mircea Eliade, *A History of Religious Ideas* , vol. 1, trans. Willard R. Trask (Chicago: The University of Chicago Press, 1978), 8–28.

22. Tattersall, 245.

23. J. A. J. Gowlett, *The Cambridge Encyclopedia*, 345.

24. Charles L. Birch and John B. Cobb, Jr., *The Liberation of Life*, 63.

25. *The Phenomenon of Man*, 185.

26. *The Cambridge Encyclopedia*, xii, 320–21.

27. "Our Hearts of Darkness: Original Sin Revisited," *Theological Studies* 49, no. 4 (December 1988): 618.

28. See Philip Hefner, *The Human Factor: Evolution, Culture and Religion* (Minneapolis: Fortress Press, 1993), 131.

29. The expression "fall upward" (see note 26, chapter 5) is used by Birch and Cobb to express the fact that the work of redemption would not restore primitive innocence but bring mature fulfillment. "In some ways," they note, "the history and culture of the human race, with all its evil, is, paradoxically, a "fall upward" (*The Liberation of Life*, 120).

30. This phrase is a proposal by Philip Hefner, *The Human Factor*, 139.

31. See note 20, chapter 3.

32. "Sin," in *A Handbook of Christian Theology*, 350. In chapter 3 we discussed the work of Catholic theologians on original sin. Many excellent Protestant studies have also been produced. The first theologian to take a truly evolutionary view, without relying on the myth of Adam's sin, was Friedrich Schleiermacher in the seventeenth century in his *The Christian Faith* (Edinburgh: T & T Clark, 1989). The definitive modern liberal Protestant exposition is that of Reinhold Niebuhr in *The Nature and Destiny of Man*, vol. 1 (New York: Charles Scribner's Sons, 1941). Niebuhr, in an existential analysis, stresses anxiety as a motivation toward sin. Marjorie Suchocki has recently published a feminist and ecological reinterpretation in *The Fall to Violence: Original Sin in Relational Theology* (New York: Continuum, 1994). She sees sin as primarily a rebellion against creation, and only secondarily as rebellion against God. Sin is "participation through intent or act in unnecessary violence that contributes to the ill-being of any aspect of earth or its inhabitants" (12).

33. See the excellent article by Francis Schüssler Fiorenza, "Redemption," *The New Dictionary of Theology*, ed. Joseph A. Komonchak, Mary Collins, and Dermot A. Lane (Collegeville, Minn.: The Liturgical Press, 1987), 836–51.

34. See Jaroslav Pelikan, *The Emergence of the Catholic Tradition (100–600)* (Chicago: The University of Chicago Press, 1971), 141–55, for early patristic theories. For an analysis of the history of the various concepts see Wolfhart Pannenberg, *Jesus–God and Man*, trans. Lewis L. Wilkins and Duane A. Priebe (Philadelphia: The Westminster Press, 1968), 39–49, 245–80, in addition to Fiorenza's article.

35. For an overview of theories of doctrinal development see William E. Reiser, S.J., *What Are They Saying About Dogma?* (New York: Paulist Press, 1978), and Thomas P. Rausch, S.J., "Development of Doctrine," in *The New Dictionary of Theology* (Collegeville, Minn.: The Liturgical Press, 1987), 280–83.

36. *Theological Investigations*, XVII, 148–54.

37. Reiser, *What Are They Saying About Dogma?* 27–33.

38. Ernan McMullin, editor, *Evolution and Creation* (Notre Dame, Ind.: University of Notre Dame Press, 1985), 2.

Bibliography

Abbott, Walter M., S.J. and Joseph Gallagher, eds. *The Documents of Vatican II*. New York: The America Press, 1966.

Alland, A. *The Human Imperative*. New York: Columbia University Press, 1972.

Allègre, Claude J. and Stephen H. Schneider. "The Evolution of the Earth." *Scientific American* (October 1994): 66–75.

Anderson, Bernard W., ed. *Creation in the Old Testament*. Philadelphia: Fortress Press, 1984.

Anselm. *St. Anselm: Basic Writings*. Trans. S. N. Deane. LaSalle, Ill.: Open Court, 1979.

Aquinas, Thomas. *Summa Contra Gentiles*. 5 vols. Trans. Anton C. Pegis, F.R.S.C. Garden City, N.Y.: Image Books, 1955.

———*Summa Theologica*. 5 vols. Trans. Fathers of the English Dominican Province. 1911; Westminster, Md.: Christian Classics, 1981.

Ardrey, Robert. *African Genesis: A Personal Investigation into the Animal Origins and the Nature of Man*. London: Collins, 1961.

Aristotle. "Metaphysics." *The Basic Works of Aristotle*. Ed. Richard McKeon. New York: Random House, 1941.

Augustine. *Basic Writings of Saint Augustine*. vol. 2. Ed. Whitney J. Oates. Trans. M. Dods, G. Wilson and J. J. Smith. Grand Rapids, Mich.: Baker Book House, 1948.

———*Against Julian*. Trans. A. Schumacher. New York: Fathers of the Church, Inc., 1957.

————*The Literal Meaning of Genesis*, 2 vols. Trans. John Taylor, S.J. New York: Newman Press, 1982.

Barbour, Ian. *Religion in an Age of Science*. New York: Harper & Row, 1990.

Baum, Gregory. "Vatican II's Constitution on Revelation: History and Interpretation." *Theological Studies* 28 (1967): 51–75.

Birch, Charles L. "Chance, Purpose, and Darwinism." *The Philosophy of Charles Hartshorne*. Ed. Lewis E. Hahn. La Salle, Ill.: Open Court, 1991.

Birch, Charles L. and John B. Cobb, Jr. *The Liberation of Life: From the Cell to the Community*. Denton, Tex.: Environmental Ethics Books, 1990.

Bracken, Joseph A., S.J. *The Triune Symbol: Persons, Process and Community*. Lanham, Md.: University Press of America, 1985.

————*Society and Spirit: A Trinitarian Cosmology*. Selinsgrove: Susquehanna University Press, 1991.

————*The Divine Matrix: Creativity as Link between East and West*. Maryknoll, New York: Orbis Books, 1995.

Brown, Peter. *Augustine of Hippo*. Berkeley and Los Angeles: University of California Press, 1967.

Brown, Raymond E., S.S., Joseph A. Fitzmyer, S.J., and Roland E. Murphy, O.Carm., eds. *The New Jerome Biblical Commentary*. Englewood Cliffs, N.J.: Prentice Hall, 1990.

Brueggemann, Walter. *Genesis*. Atlanta: John Knox Press, 1982.

Burns, J. Patout, S.J. *Theological Anthropology*. Philadelphia: Fortress Press, 1981.

Calvin, John. *Institutes of the Christian Religion*. 2 vols. Ed. John T. McNeill. Trans. Ford Lewis Battles. Philadelphia: The Westminster Press, 1960.

————*Commentaries on the Epistle of Paul the Apostle to the Romans*. Trans. and ed. Rev. John Owen. Grand Rapids, Mich.: Baker Book House, 1996.

Calvin, William H. "The Emergence of Intelligence." *Scientific American* (October 1994): 100–07.

Catechism of the Catholic Church. Mahwah, N.J.: Paulist Press, 1994.

Clifford, Anne M. "Postmodern Scientific Cosmology and the

Christian God of Creation." *Horizons* 21, no. 1 (Spring 1994): 62–84.

Cobb, John B., Jr. *Matters of Life and Death*. Louisville, Kentucky: Westminster/John Knox Press, 1991.

Cobb, John B., Jr. and David Ray Griffin. *Process Theology: An Introductory Exposition*. Philadelphia: The Westminster Press, 1976.

Conner, James L., S.J. "Original Sin: Contemporary Approaches." *Theological Studies* 29 (1968): 215–40.

Danto, Arthur C. "Persons." *The Encyclopedia of Philosophy*. 6 vols. Ed. Paul Edwards. New York: Macmillan Publishing Co., 1967.

De Duve, Christian. *Vital Dust: Life as a Cosmic Imperative*. New York: HarperCollins, 1995.

Duffy, Stephen J. "Our Hearts of Darkness: Original Sin Revisited." *Theological Studies* 49 (1988): 597–622.

Edey, Maitland A. and Donald C. Johanson. *Blueprints: Solving the Mystery of Evolution*. Boston: Little, Brown and Company, 1989.

Eliade, Mircea. *A History of Religious Ideas*. Vol. 1. Trans. Willard R. Trask. Chicago: The University of Chicago Press, 1978.

Fairweather, Eugene R., ed. and trans. *A Scholastic Miscellany: Anselm to Ockham*. Philadelphia: The Westminster Press, 1956.

Ferris, Timothy. *Coming of Age in the Milky Way*. New York: William Morrow and Company, 1988.

———. *The Whole Shebang: A State-of-the Universe(s) Report*. New York: Simon & Schuster, 1997.

Flannery, Austin, O.P., ed. *Vatican Council II: The Conciliar and Post Conciliar Documents*. 2 vols. Northport, N.Y.: Costello Publishing Company, 1975 & 1982.

Gehrels, Tom. "Collisions with Comets and Asteroids." *Scientific American* (March 1996): 54–59.

Gilson, Etienne. *The Christian Philosophy of Saint Augustine*. New York: Random House, 1960.

Goudge, Thomas A. "Evolutionism." *Dictionary of the History of Ideas*. Ed. Philip P. Wiener. New York: Charles Scribner's Sons, 1973.

Gould, Stephen Jay. *Wonderful Life: The Burgess Shale and the Nature of History*. New York: W. W. Norton & Company, 1989.

Graff, Ann O'Hara, ed. *In the Embrace of God: Feminist Approaches to Theological Anthropology*. Maryknoll, N.Y.: Orbis Books, 1995.

Griffin, David Ray. "What Is Consciousness and Why Is It So Problematic?" Claremont, Calif.: The Center for Process Studies, February 13, 1992.

Haag, Herbert. *Is Original Sin in Scripture?* Trans. Dorothy Thompson. New York: Sheed and Ward, 1969.

Hartshorne, Charles. *The Divine Relativity: A Social Concept of God*. New Haven: Yale University Press, 1948.

————*The Logic of Perfection and Other Essays in Neoclassical Metaphysics*. LaSalle: Open Court, 1962.

————*Creative Synthesis and Philosophic Method*. 1970; Lanham, Md.: University Press of America, 1983.

————*Omnipotence and Other Theological Mistakes*. Albany: The State University of New York Press, 1984.

Hartshorne, Charles and William L. Reese. *Philosophers Speak of God*. Chicago: The University of Chicago Press, 1953.

Haught, John F. *The Cosmic Adventure: Science, Religion and the Quest for Purpose*. New York: Paulist Press, 1984.

————*Science and Religion: From Conflict to Conversation*. New York: Paulist Press, 1995.

Hawkings, Stephen. *A Brief History of Time: From the Big Bang to Black Holes*. New York: Bantam Books, 1988.

Hayes, Zachary, O.F.M. *What Are They Saying About Creation?* New York: Paulist Press, 1980.

Hefner, Philip. *The Human Factor: Evolution, Culture and Religion*. Minn.: Fortress Press, 1993.

Hulsbosch, A., O.S.A. *God in Creation and Evolution*. Trans. Martin Versfeld. New York: Sheed and Ward, 1965.

Johanson, Donald and James Shreeve. *Lucy's Child: The Discovery of a Human Ancestor*. New York: William Morrow, 1989.

Jones, Steve, Robert Martin, and David Pilbeam, eds. *The Cambridge Encyclopedia of Human Evolution*. Cambridge, Cambridge University Press, 1992.

Jung, Carl G. *The Undiscovered Self*. Trans. R. F. C. Hull. Boston: Little, Brown and Company, 1957.

Kauffman, Stuart. *At Home in the Universe: The Search of the Laws of*

Self-Organization and Complexity. New York: Oxford University Press, 1995.

Kelly, J. N. D. *Early Christian Doctrines.* San Francisco: HarperCollins Publishers, 1978.

Komonchak, Joseph A., Mary Collins, and Dermot A. Lane, eds. *The New Dictionary of Theology.* Collegeville, Minn.: The Liturgical Press, 1987.

Korsmeyer, Jerry D. *God–Creature–Revelation: A Neoclassical Framework for Fundamental Theology.* Lanham, Md.: University Press of America, 1995.

Kuper, Adam. *The Chosen Primate: Human Nature and Cultural Diversity.* Cambridge, Mass.: Harvard University Press, 1994.

Leakey, R. E. and R. Lewin. *Origins: What New Discoveries Reveal About the Emergence of Our Species and Its Possible Future.* London: Macdonald & Jane's, 1977.

———*Origins Reconsidered: In Search of What Makes Us Human.* New York: Doubleday, 1992.

Lessem, Don. *Dinosaurs Rediscovered: New Findings Which Are Revolutionizing Dinosaur Science.* New York: Touchstone, 1992.

Lonergan, Anne and Caroline Richards, eds. *Thomas Berry and the New Cosmology.* Mystic, Conn.: Twenty-Third Publications, 1987.

Lovejoy, Arthur O. *The Great Chain of Being: A Study of the History of an Idea.* Cambridge, Mass.: Harvard University Press, 1936.

Luther, Martin. *Martin Luther: Selections from His Writings.* Ed. John Dillenberger. Garden City, N.Y.: Doubleday and Company, 1961.

———*The Library of Christian Classics.* Vol. 12. Ed. and trans. Wilhelm Pauck. Philadelphia: The Westminster Press, 1961.

MacLean, Paul D. *A Triune Concept of the Brain and Behavior.* Toronto: University of Toronto Press, 1973.

———"Women: A More Balanced Brain?" *Zygon* 31, no. 3 (September 1996): 421–39.

McDermott, Brian O., S.J. "Original Sin: Recent Developments." *Theological Studies* 38 (1977): 478–512.

McMullin, Ernan, ed. *Evolution and Creation.* Notre Dame, Ind.: University of Notre Dame Press, 1985.

Menzies, Allen, ed. *Ante-Nicene Fathers*, 10 vols. 1896; Peabody, Mass.: Hendrickson Publishers, Inc., 1994.

Metz, Johannes, ed. *The Evolving World and Theology*. New York: Paulist Press, 1967.

Meyendorff, John. *Byzantine Theology: Historical Trends and Doctrinal Themes*. New York: Fordham University Press, 1974.

Nemesszeghy, Ervin, S.J. and John Russell, S.J. *Theology of Evolution*. Butler, Wis.: Clergy Book Service, 1971.

Neuner, J., S.J. and J. Dupuis, S.J., eds. *The Christian Faith in the Doctrinal Documents of the Catholic Church*. New York: Alba House, 1982.

Niebuhr, Reinhold. *The Nature and Destiny of Man*. Vol. 1. New York: Charles Scribner's Sons, 1941.

——"Sin." *A Handbook of Christian Theology*. Ed. Marvin Halverson and Arthur A. Cohen. New York: World Publishing, 1958.

Numbers, Ronald L. *The Creationists: The Evolution of Scientific Creationism*. Berkeley and Los Angeles: University of California Press, 1992.

Ong, Walter J, S.J. "Do We Live in a Post-Christian Age?" *America* (February 3, 1996): 18.

Orgel, Leslie E. "The Origin of Life on Earth." *Scientific American* (October 1994): 77–83.

Orsy, Ladislas, S.J. "Review of Francis A. Sullivan, S.J.'s *Creative Fidelity: Weighing and Interpreting Documents of the Magisterium*." *Theological Studies* 58, no.1 (March 1997): 178.

O'Collins, Gerald, S.J. *Retrieving Fundamental Theology: The Three Styles of Contemporary Theology*. New York: Paulist Press, 1993.

O'Donovan, Leo, S.J. "Was Vatican II Evolutionary? A Note on Conciliar Language." *Theological Studies* 36 (1975): 495.

Pagels, Elaine. *Adam, Eve, and the Serpent*. New York: Vintage Books, 1988.

Pannenberg, Wolfhart. *Jesus–God and Man*. Trans. Lewis L.Wilkins and Duane A. Priebe. Philadelphia: The Westminster Press, 1968.

Pelikan, Jaroslav. *The Emergence of the Catholic Tradition (100–600)*. Chicago: The University of Chicago Press, 1971.

Phan, Peter. "Contemporary Contexts and Issues in Eschatology." *Theological Studies* 55, no. 3 (September 1994): 335–36.

Piaget, Jean. *Behavior and Evolution.* Trans. Donald Nicholson-Smith. London: Routledge & Kegan Paul, 1979.

Plato. *Timaeus.* Ed. Francis M. Cornford. New York: The Bobbs-Merrill Company, 1959.

Polkinghorne, John. *The Faith of a Physicist: Reflections of a Bottom-Up Thinker.* Princeton: Princeton University Press, 1994.

Pontifical Biblical Commission. "The Interpretation of the Bible in the Church." *Origins* 23, no. 29 (January 6, 1994).

Portalié, Eugene, S.J. *A Guide to the Thought of Saint Augustine.* Trans. R. J. Bastian. Chicago: Henry Regnery Company, 1960.

Rahner, Karl, S.J. *Hominisation: The Evolutionary Origin of Man as a Theological Problem.* Trans. W. J. O'Hara. 1958; New York: Herder and Herder, 1965.

———*Theological Investigations.* Vol. 17. Trans. Margaret Kohl. New York: Crossroad, 1981.

———*Foundations of Christian Faith: An Introduction to the Idea of Christianity.* Trans. William V. Dyck. New York: Crossroad, 1984.

———*Theological Investigations.* Vol. 21. Trans. Hugh M. Riley. New York: Crossroad, 1988.

Rahner, Karl, S.J., ed. *Encyclopedia of Theology: The Concise Sacramentum Mundi.* New York: Crossroad, 1982.

Ratzinger, J. Cardinal and Christoph Schönborn. *Introduction to the Catechism of the Catholic Church.* San Francisco: Ignatius Press, 1994.

Reiser, William E., S.J., *What Are They Saying About Dogma?* New York: Paulist Press, 1978.

Ricoeur, Paul. *The Symbolism of Evil.* Trans. Emerson Buchanan. Boston: Beacon Press, 1967.

Rondet, Henri, S.J. *Original Sin: The Patristic and Theological Background.* Trans. Cajetan Finegan, O.P. Staten Island, N.Y.: Alba House, 1972.

Ruether, Rosemary Radford. *Sexism and God-Talk: Toward a Feminist Theology.* Boston: Beacon Press, 1983.

Russell, R. J., W. R. Stoeger, S.J., and G. V. Coyne, S.J., eds. *Physics,*

Philosophy and Theology: A Common Quest for Understanding.
Vatican Observatory: Libreria Editrice Vaticana, 1988.

Russell, Robert John, Nancey Murphy, and C. J. Isham, eds.
Quantum Cosmology and the Laws of Nature: Scientific Perspectives on Divine Action. Vatican City State: Vatican Observatory Publications, 1993.

Sagan, Carl. *The Dragons of Eden: Speculations on the Evolution of Human Intelligence.* New York: Random House, 1977.

————"The Search for Extraterrestrial Life." *Scientific American* (October 1994): 92–99.

————*The Demon-Haunted World: Science as a Candle in the Dark.* New York: Random House, 1995.

Sagan, Carl and Ann Druyan, *Shadows of Forgotten Ancestors: A Search for Who We Are.* New York: Random House, 1992.

Schaff, Philip, ed. *Nicene and Post-Nicene Fathers.* First Series, 14 vols. Peabody, Mass.: Hendrickson Publishers, Inc., 1994.

Schaff, Philip and Henry Wace, eds. *Nicene and Post-Nicene Fathers.* Second Series, 14 vols. Peabody Mass.: Hendrickson Publishers, Inc., 1995.

Schoonenberg, Peter, S.J. *God's World in the Making.* Pittsburgh, Pa.: Duquesne University Press, 1964.

Scullion, John J. *Genesis: A Commentary for Students, Teachers, and Preachers.* Collegeville, Minn.: The Liturgical Press, 1992.

Speiser, E. A. *Genesis.* Garden City, N.Y.: Doubleday and Company, 1981.

Spicq, Ceslaus, O.P. *Agape in the New Testament.* 3 vols. Trans. Sister Marie Aquinas McNamara, O.P. and Sister Mary Honoria Richter, O.P. St. Louis: B. Herder Book Co., 1963, 1965, 1966.

Suchocki, Marjorie Hewett. *The End of Evil: Process Eschatology in Historical Context.* New York: The State University of New York Press, 1988.

————*The Fall to Violence: Original Sin in Relational Theology.* New York: Continuum, 1994.

Sullivan, Francis A., S.J. *Creative Fidelity: Weighing and Interpreting Documents of the Magisterium.* New York: Paulist Press, 1996.

Tattersall, Ian. *The Fossil Trail: How We Know What We Think We*

Know About Human Evolution. New York: Oxford University Press, 1995.

Teilhard de Chardin, Pierre. *The Phenomenon of Man*. Trans. Bernard Wall. 1955; New York: Harper & Brothers, 1959.

————*Christianity and Evolution*. Trans. René Hague. New York: Harcourt Brace Jovanovich, Inc., 1971.

Tracy, David. *Blessed Rage for Order*. New York: Seabury, 1975.

Vandervelde, George. *Original Sin: Two Contemporary Roman Catholic Approaches*. Washington, D.C.: University of America Press, 1981.

Vawter, Bruce. *On Genesis*. Garden City, N.Y.: Doubleday, 1977.

Von Rad, Gerhard. *Genesis*. Philadelphia: The Westminster Press, 1972.

Walsh, Michael J., ed. *Commentary on the Catechism of the Catholic Church*. Collegeville, Minn.: Liturgical Press, 1994.

Weishampel, David B., Peter Dodson, and Halszka Osmólska, eds. *The Dinosauria*. Berkeley: University of California Press, 1990.

Westermann, Claus. *Creation*. Trans. John J. Scullion, S.J., Philadelphia: Fortress Press, 1974.

White, Frank. *The Overview Effect: Space Exploration and Human Evolution*. Boston: Houghton Mifflin Company, 1987.

Whitehead, Alfred North. *Process and Reality, Corrected Edition*. Ed. D. R. Griffin and D. W. Sherburne. 1929; New York: The Free Press, 1978.

Whitney, Barry L. *Evil and the Process God*. New York: The Edwin Mellen Press, 1985.

————*What Are They Saying About God and Evil?* New York: Paulist Press, 1989.

Williams, Daniel Day. *The Spirit and the Forms of Love*. New York: Harper & Row, 1968.

Wilson, Edward O. *Sociobiology: The New Synthesis*. Cambridge, Mass.: The Belknap Press of Harvard University Press, 1975.

————*On Human Nature*. London: Harvard University Press, 1978.

————*The Diversity of Life*. Cambridge, Mass.: The Belnap Press of Harvard University Press, 1992.

Index